HOME REPAIR AND IMPROVEMENT

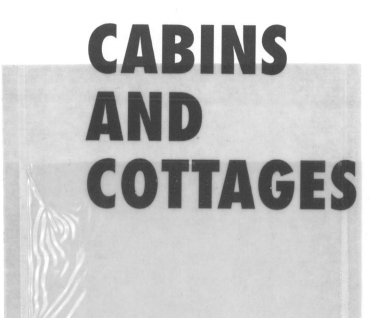

CABINS
AND
COTTAGES

OTHER PUBLICATIONS:

DO IT YOURSELF
The Time-Life Complete Gardener
Home Repair and Improvement
The Art of Woodworking
Fix It Yourself

COOKING
Weight Watchers® Smart Choice Recipe Collection
Great Taste/Low Fat
Williams-Sonoma Kitchen Library

HISTORY
The American Story
Voices of the Civil War
The American Indians
Lost Civilizations
Mysteries of the Unknown
Time Frame
The Civil War
Cultural Atlas

TIME-LIFE KIDS
Library of First Questions and Answers
A Child's First Library of Learning
I Love Math
Nature Company Discoveries
Understanding Science & Nature

SCIENCE/NATURE
Voyage Through the Universe

For information on and a full description
of any of the Time-Life Books series listed above,
please call 1-800-621-7026 or write:

Reader Information
Time-Life Customer Service
P.O. Box C-32068
Richmond Virginia 23261-2068

HOME REPAIR AND IMPROVEMENT

CABINS AND COTTAGES

BY THE EDITORS OF TIME-LIFE BOOKS, ALEXANDRIA, VIRGINIA

The Consultants

Gary D. Cook has had a dual appointment since 1980 as Energy Extension Specialist for Building Construction (IFAS) and Assistant Professor (School of Building Construction) at the University of Florida. An authority on building energy efficiency, Professor Cook has written a book on insulation.

Richard Day spent eight years with the Portland Cement Association as a writer and editor on subjects relating to concrete. Based in southern California, he has built three houses and authored several books on concrete, masonry, and plumbing.

Wally Neighbors has two Technical Engineering degrees from Purdue University and is Manager of Customer Services at Flint and Walling Pump Inc. of Kendallville, Indiana. He is an authority on pumps, wells, and pressure relief valves.

Mike Senty is the owner and operator of Senty Log Homes in Grand Marais, Minnesota. Based on centuries of tradition, his work can be found at numerous executive log retreats and resorts across the midwest. Mr. Senty serves on the Board of Directors of the Great Lakes Logcrafters Association.

Mark M. Steele is a professional home inspector in the Washington, D.C., area. He has developed and conducted training programs in home-ownership skills for first-time homeowners. He appears frequently on television and radio as an expert in home repair and consumer topics.

CONTENTS

Getting Started

Before you can begin building a vacation home, you will need to prepare the site. In the absence of heavy machinery such as bulldozers or tractors, tools like chain saws and comealongs can substantially lighten the work of felling trees and removing logs and boulders. When the area is cleared, you can begin construction by laying a foundation that suits the site and type of structure you plan to build.

Nailing a band joist to a header joist →

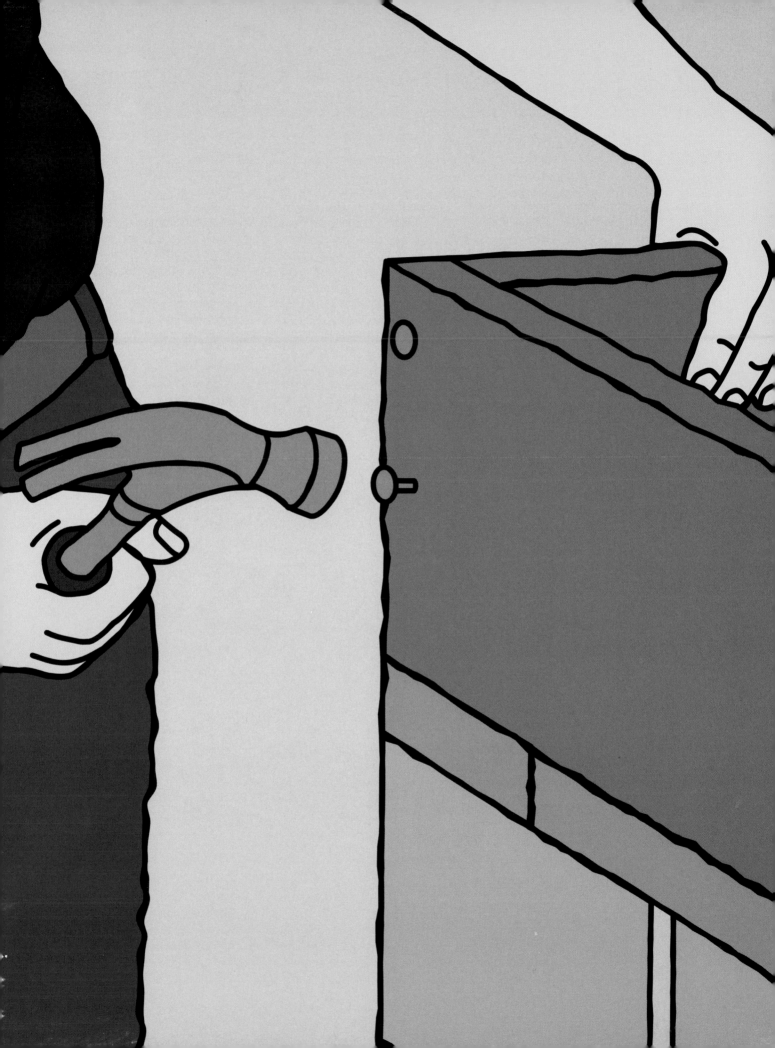

Electricity is indispensable during the construction of a vacation home, either to power electric tools or to recharge the batteries of cordless models. If the building site is close to power lines, you can have the utility company install a temporary power drop; if it lies miles from electric lines, a portable generator can produce electricity on the spot, and can become a permanent feature once the structure is built.

Portable Generators: The smallest practical unit for powering portable tools has a generating capacity of 2,000 watts, enough to run a $7\frac{1}{4}$-inch circular saw. If you plan to use stationary tools, you'll need one that can produce about 3,500 watts. When your building plans include a well with an electric pump *(pages 107-114)*, obtain a unit that generates 4,000 watts or more, and install it in a permanent, sheltered location. Consider a model that can be switched from 120 to 240 volts to supply the current necessary to run a submersible pump. A unit that supplies up to 7,000 watts can operate additional electric devices such as lights or a refrigerator.

A Temporary Power Drop: Consisting of an electric meter, a weatherproof service panel, and weatherproof receptacles, a power drop mounts on a pole or at any location convenient to the site. Choose a location that will be out of the way during construction, but one that is close enough that you do not need to string extension cords together or extend wires to reach the building. When the time comes, it will be simple to move the meter and panel or extend wires from the power drop to the cabin or cottage.

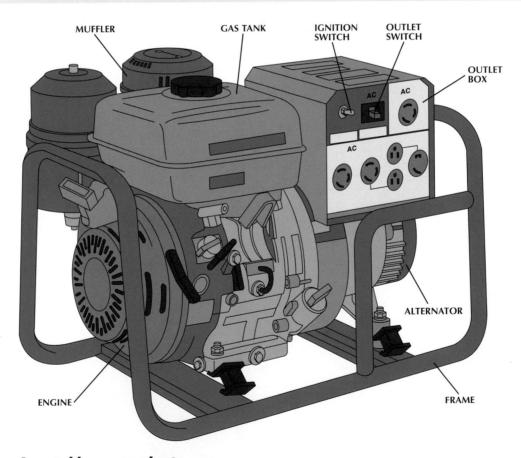

MUFFLER   GAS TANK   IGNITION SWITCH   OUTLET SWITCH   OUTLET BOX   ALTERNATOR   FRAME   ENGINE

A portable power plant.

A typical generator consists of a gas-powered engine that drives an alternator to produce the standard 120-volt alternating current. The power is made available through receptacles in an outlet box; an outlet switch turns power to the receptacles on and off. The components are attached to a frame fitted with carrying handles. The engine requires about the same maintenance as that of a lawn mower—periodic replenishment and replacement of oil, and an occasional new spark plug.

Once you have chosen an appropriate site for your vacation retreat *(pages 93-94)*, you'll need to remove underbrush, trees, and boulders from the area. This can be a formidable task, but it is mostly a matter of picking the right tool for each job and using it simply and safely.

Clearing Vegetation: Cut bushes down to ground level with a pair of pruning shears, and dig the roots up with a shovel the same way you would those of a small tree *(page 14)*. Clear tall grass and vines with a gas-powered trimmer; or use a scythe or a hand sickle, always holding your free hand away from the blade.

Removing Trees: Felling large, mature trees is a relatively complex operation, but a chain saw can put the job within anyone's reach *(pages 10-11)*. Until you are experienced at working with a power saw, however, restrict your efforts to trunks whose diameter is less than the length of the saw blade. It is easier to fell a tree in the direction of its natural lean, but this may not always be possible. You can direct a tree away from its natural lean using wedges and a tapered hinge cut in the trunk *(page 12)*.

Removing Rocks: For stones that are too large for you to budge, wrap rope or a chain around them and use a comealong *(page 13)*. Or, split them into smaller pieces that can be moved more easily: Fit a drill with a masonry bit and bore holes in the rocks, then drive in steel wedges with a sledgehammer until the rocks break apart.

 *Before you start cutting any tree, plan an escape* **CAUTION** *route—ideally at about a 45-degree angle from the proposed direction of the fall—and remove all obstacles from the path.*

 TOOLS

Chain saw
Sledgehammer
Wooden wedges

SAFETY TIPS

Put on a hard hat, goggles or a face shield, hearing protection, work gloves, and steel-toed boots when working with a chain saw.

A LIGHTWEIGHT CHAIN SAW

In addition to severing tree trunks and branches, a lightweight chain saw can double as an all-purpose wood-cutting tool. Although not as powerful as a heavy-duty model *(pages 10-12)*, and therefore unable to cut larger trunks, a lightweight saw can weigh up to 4 pounds less, making it easier to handle.

ANGLED
CUT

DIRECTION
OF FALL

1. Cutting a notch in the trunk.

◆ On the side of the tree that faces the direction of its natural lean, hold a chain saw with the blade angled at 45 degrees to the trunk.

◆ Turn on the engine, let it come to full throttle, and make an angled cut about one-third of the way through the trunk. Pull the blade from the cut.

◆ Holding the blade horizontally at the bottom of the angled cut, saw to the end of the cut (*left*). Retract the blade and push the wedge-shaped piece from the notch.

CHAIN-SAW SAFETY GEAR

If you are clearing away a large number of trees with a chain saw, it is a good idea to wear special safety clothing. Leg coverings, or "chaps," as well as the boots and gloves, are lined with a protective material that is reinforced to resist being cut through. The helmet incorporates ear protection and a face shield.

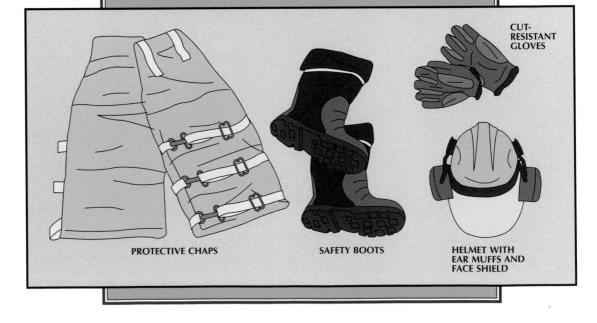

CUT-
RESISTANT
GLOVES

PROTECTIVE CHAPS   SAFETY BOOTS   HELMET WITH
EAR MUFFS AND
FACE SHIELD

2. Making the felling cut.

◆ On the side of the trunk opposite the notch, start a horizontal cut 2 inches above the bottom of the notch *(right)*.
◆ Stop cutting when the blade is 2 to 3 inches from the back of the notch, creating a hinge *(inset)*. The trunk will pivot on the hinge, and the tree should fall. If not, drive in wedges *(page 12, bottom)*.

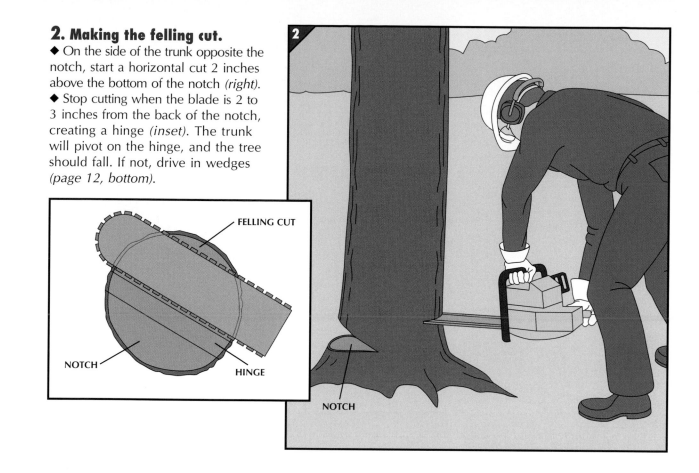

CUTTING A LARGE TRUNK

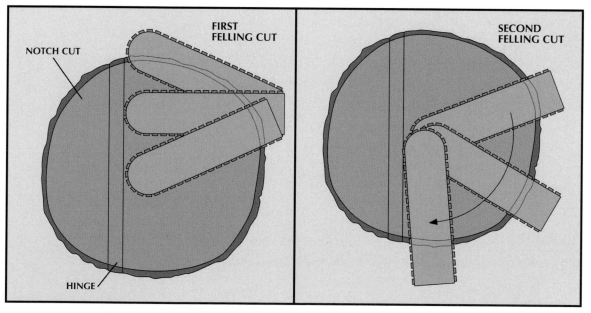

Making two felling cuts.

To fell a tree whose diameter is one to two times the length of the chain-saw blade, make two felling cuts.
◆ Start with a notch cut *(opposite, Step 1)*, then make the first felling cut by holding your body stationary and pivoting the saw through about half the trunk, leaving a 2-inch hinge between the felling cut and the notch cut *(above, left)*.
◆ To make the next felling cut, place the saw at the end of the preceding cut and walk the blade around the tree, stopping 2 inches before the notch to leave a hinge *(above, right)*. If the tree does not fall, drive wedges into the felling cuts *(page 12, bottom)*.

FELLING TREES IN DIFFICULT SITUATIONS

Felling a sharply leaning tree.

◆ As shown in the inset, a series of cuts is necessary to fell a tree that leans sharply. First, make shallow cuts on each side of the trunk parallel to the direction of fall *(right)* to prevent the tree from splitting behind the notch cut.

◆ At the same level as the side cuts—but perpendicular to them—cut a notch halfway into the trunk *(page 10, Step 1)*.

◆ Finally, make the felling cut *(page 11, Step 2)*.

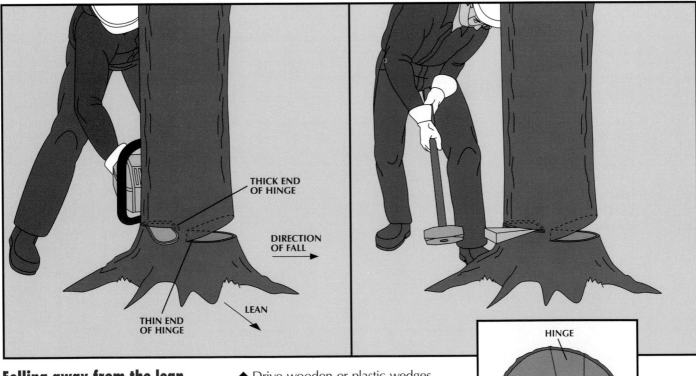

Felling away from the lean.

◆ Cut a notch on the side of the tree facing the direction that you want the tree to fall *(page 10, Step 1)*.

◆ For the felling cut *(page 11, Step 2)*, angle the chain-saw blade so the hinge will be thicker opposite the natural direction of the lean, then make the cut *(above, left)*.

◆ Drive wooden or plastic wedges into the felling cut near the thin side of the hinge *(above, right, and inset)*; the wedges will force the tree upward on that side, shifting its center of gravity away from the lean. If driving in the wedges does not cause the tree to fall, drive in thicker wedges.

Once large trees are cut down, you can maneuver the logs around your building site with a hand-operated comealong. Rather than chopping down small trees and then getting rid of the roots, you can uproot them *(page 14)*, then either dispose of them or replant them somewhere else on the site.

Transplanting Trees: If you opt for transplanting, keep in mind that trees taller than 10 feet with trunks that are greater than 3 inches thick will be unwieldy to move and will be less likely to survive when replanted. A tree's chances are greatest if you transplant in a period of low growth activity—in spring before leaves appear, or in autumn after they fall.

Moving Logs: The comealong, a tool with a ratchet mechanism and a lever that is moved back and forth to reel in a cable, gives you the mechanical advantage needed to clear out heavy logs by hand *(below)*.

Removing Stumps: For trees that were already cut down, uproot small stumps the same way you would a small tree; larger ones can be ground down to below grade using a rented stump grinder *(page 14)*. For very large stumps, it's best to hire a professional to remove them.

TOOLS

Heavy-duty chains
Hook for chain
Comealong
Flat spade

SAFETY TIPS

Wear steel-toed safety boots when moving logs.

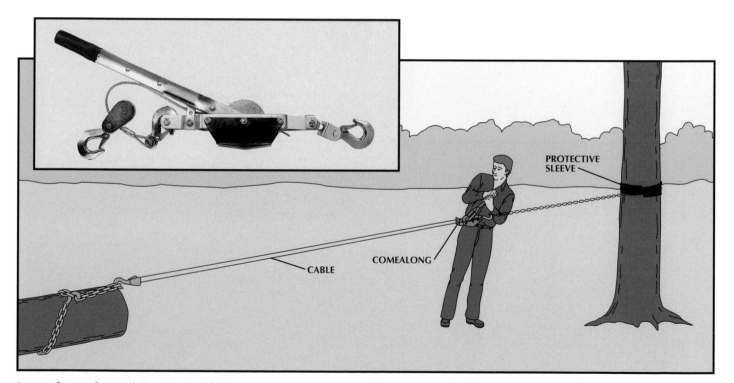

PROTECTIVE SLEEVE

COMEALONG

CABLE

Dragging a log with a comealong.
◆ Wrap a heavy-duty chain with a hook around the log, about 2 feet from the end, using the hook to hold the chain in place.
◆ Fasten a second chain, without a hook, around the trunk of a tree in the direction you want to pull the log. Unless you will be cutting down this tree, protect the bark with a sleeve, such as a bicycle inner tube.
◆ Hook the extendable cable of a comealong *(photo-graph)* to the chain on the log, and hook the stationary end to the chain around the tree.
◆ Draw the log toward the tree by moving the handle on the comealong back and forth *(above)*.
◆ Release the tension mechanism on the comealong, remove the chain from the tree, attach it to another tree further along, and repeat the process as many times as necessary to move the log off the building site.

Removing the rootball.

◆ Using a flat spade with a sharp blade, slice through the roots in a 30- to 36-inch-wide circle around the trunk. Push the blade into the ground at about a 30-degree angle toward the trunk to taper the root ball for easy removal *(right)*.

◆ Dig a 24- to 30-inch-deep access trench around the rootball.

◆ Sever the taproot—the root section that heads straight down into the ground—and any other uncut roots under the tree with the spade. With a helper, lift out the tree and rootball.

TAPROOT

ROOTBALL

A PORTABLE STUMP CUTTER

An alternative to the labor-intensive process of chopping or digging up stumps is to rent a stump cutter. This gas-powered machine has an angled blade that shaves a stump down to ground level quickly and easily. On some models, the handlebars can be attached to a holder at one end of the tool, as shown here, or to a longer holder at the other end, to allow the cutter to reach stumps near obstructions. A tough rubber flap deflects chips away from the operator, but be sure to wear goggles when you are running the machine.

From a distance, a cottage resting on wooden poles may look shaky and fragile. In reality, such a foundation can provide decades of stalwart support and withstand storms and floods.

Site Suitability: Pole platforms cannot be used everywhere. In some localities, building codes require continuous-wall foundations *(pages 24-28)*. Walls are also recommended in earthquake-prone regions, cold climates, and on building sites with insecure soil—such as sand or soft clay—or a slope greater than 1 in 10—1 foot of rise for every 10 horizontal feet. The techniques on these pages are designed only for fairly level sites with stable soil.

Lumber and Concrete: Buy pressure-treated poles that are reasonably straight and uniform in diameter, and get enough to space them about 8 feet apart. For a level site, they need to be long enough to extend $1\frac{1}{2}$ to 3 feet above ground level and at least 4 feet below it, or at least 6 inches below the frost line if it is deeper than 4 feet. Where the ground slopes gently, buy poles that are 1 foot longer. For the beams, obtain pressure-treated lumber long enough to span the rows of poles.

To anchor poles in their holes *(page 16, Step 2)*, you will need concrete or a wet mixture of 1 part Portland cement to 5 parts clean soil, free of roots, leaves, and other organic matter. Prepare this mixture by combining the dry ingredients, then adding slightly less water than you would for concrete—the amount of water will vary depending on the soil.

TOOLS

Maul
Hammer
Tape measure (50-foot)
Plumb bob
Power auger
Garden spade
Posthole digger
Carpenter's level
Line level
2 x 4 tamper
Bucksaw
Electric drill with auger bit ($\frac{1}{2}$")
Wrench
Circular saw

MATERIALS

1 x 2s, 1 x 6s
2 x 4s, 2 x 8s
Pressure-treated poles (6"-8" thick)
Pressure-treated 2 x 6s, 2 x 10s
Exterior-grade plywood ($\frac{3}{4}$")
Ring-shank nails (2")
Galvanized common nails ($2\frac{1}{2}$", 3")
Multipurpose framing anchors and nails
Carriage bolts ($\frac{1}{2}$"), washers, and nuts
Powdered chalk
Concrete mix or Portland cement and clean soil

SAFETY TIPS

Goggles protect your eyes when you are using power tools or hammering. Wear gloves when handling pressure-treated wood; add a dust mark when cutting it.

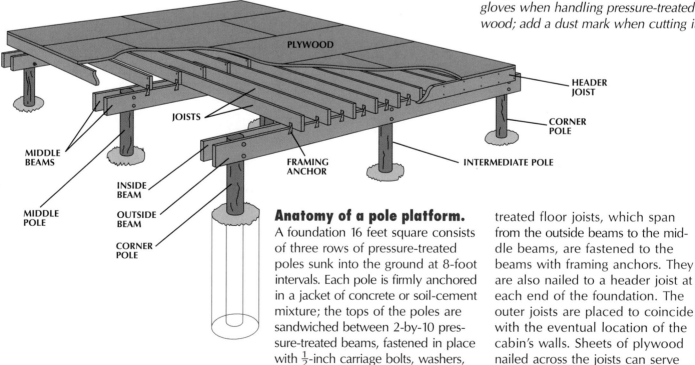

PLYWOOD

HEADER JOIST

CORNER POLE

INTERMEDIATE POLE

JOISTS

FRAMING ANCHOR

MIDDLE BEAMS

INSIDE BEAM

OUTSIDE BEAM

CORNER POLE

MIDDLE POLE

Anatomy of a pole platform.
A foundation 16 feet square consists of three rows of pressure-treated poles sunk into the ground at 8-foot intervals. Each pole is firmly anchored in a jacket of concrete or soil-cement mixture; the tops of the poles are sandwiched between 2-by-10 pressure-treated beams, fastened in place with $\frac{1}{2}$-inch carriage bolts, washers, and nuts. The 2-by-6 pressure-treated floor joists, which span from the outside beams to the middle beams, are fastened to the beams with framing anchors. They are also nailed to a header joist at each end of the foundation. The outer joists are placed to coincide with the eventual location of the cabin's walls. Sheets of plywood nailed across the joists can serve as a subfloor or as a finish floor.

PUTTING UP A POLE PLATFORM

1. Digging the holes.

◆ Lay out the site as you would for a block wall *(pages 24-25, Steps 1-3)*, marking the location of the poles in relation to the walls.

◆ Rent a power auger to dig each posthole to a depth of 4 feet or at least 6 inches below the frost line, whichever is deeper. You can use a one-man power auger *(photograph)*, but a two-man version *(right)* is more powerful and easier to handle.

◆ With a spade and a clamshell posthole digger, widen the holes to 16 to 18 inches in diameter.

◆ Set all the poles in their holes.

On a gently sloping site—one with a rise of 1 in 10 or less—you will need to dig the postholes deeper and larger than those on a level site; consult local building codes or a building professional.

POLE LOCATION

1 x 2

STAKE

LINE LEVEL

2. Setting the poles.

◆ Plumb the corner poles with a level and, while a helper holds them straight, brace them with 1-by-2s nailed to stakes.

◆ Measure down from the top of one corner pole the width of a beam plus 3 inches, and make a mark there. Drive a nail at the mark.

◆ Stretch a string fitted with a line level from the nail to the other corner post, and mark the second corner post at the height of the level string. Drive a nail there and tie the string to it.

◆ Align the middle pole with the string, then plumb and brace it *(above)*. Mark the point where the string touches the pole.

◆ Prepare enough concrete or cement-soil mixture to fill in around the poles and shovel it into each hole, overfilling it slightly. Tamp the mixture with a 2-by-4, sloping the top downward from the pole to the ground.

◆ Repeat the process on the other rows of poles, then remove the strings and nails and let the concrete cure for a day.

Working with Concrete in the Wilderness

To save you the trouble of having to mix separate ingredients for concrete—Portland cement, sand, and gravel—get the cement and sand premixed. Since the site is unlikely to have shelter during the early stages of construction, protect the dry ingredients by placing the bags on wooden pallets and covering them with plastic sheets or tarpaulins. To clean up your tools after a day's work without the luxury of running water, keep a 6-gallon bucket of water on hand, and when you're finished with a tool, place it in the bucket. Replace the water as necessary, but use it to clean out the wheelbarrow before discarding it.

3. Starting the daps.

To enable the beams to sit squarely against the poles, you'll need to cut a notch, called a dap, on both sides of each pole near the top. With a bucksaw or pruning saw, first make a series of horizontal cuts $1\frac{1}{2}$ inches wide and $\frac{1}{8}$ to $\frac{1}{4}$ inch deep on one side of the pole *(right)*. Work from the top of the pole to the mark you made in Step 2.

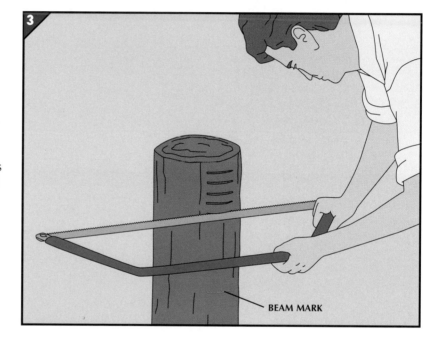

BEAM MARK

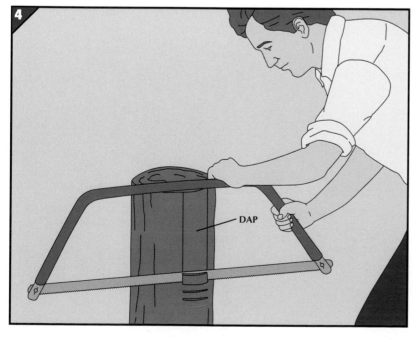

DAP

4. Finishing the daps.

◆ Place the saw on top of the pole and align the blade with the ends of the horizontal cuts on one side, then saw down through the cuts from the top of the pole to the beam mark *(left)*.
◆ Cut daps on the same side of the remaining poles.

5. Locating the outside beams.

◆ With a helper, set a beam against the outside of one row of poles so the bottom edge sits squarely in the daps in the posts.

◆ Holding the beam level, temporarily fasten it to each pole with a 3-inch common nail *(left)*.

◆ Nail a beam to the outsides of each remaining row of poles in the same way.

◆ Cut the tops of the poles flush with the tops of the beams.

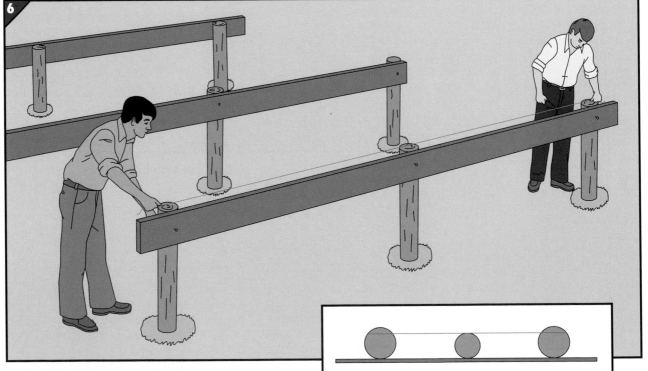

6. Positioning the inside beams.

◆ With a helper, run a string across a row of poles on the side opposite the beam *(above)*.

◆ Line up the string with the edge of the pole that is smallest in diameter *(inset)*.

◆ Mark the tops of the larger poles at the string line, and cut a dap *(page 17, Steps 3 and 4)* at each mark.

◆ Temporarily nail beams to the inside of the poles as described above.

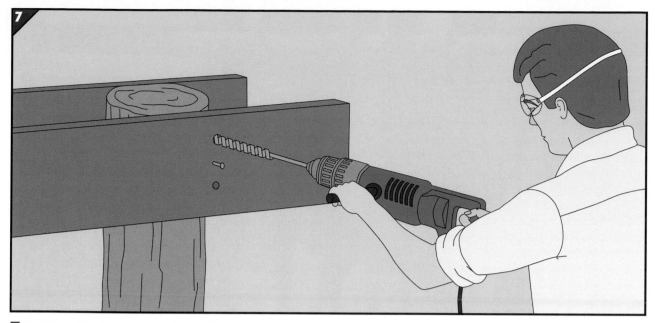

7. Bolting the beams to the poles.

◆ Measure and mark a point one-third of the way from the top and bottom of each beam.
◆ Install a $\frac{1}{2}$-inch auger bit in an electric drill and bore a hole through the beams and pole at each mark *(above)*.
◆ Insert a $\frac{1}{2}$-inch carriage bolt about 1 inch longer than the combined thickness of the beams and pole into each hole.
◆ Tighten washers and nuts onto the bolts.

As wood tends to shrink over time, check the nuts for tightness several weeks after the foundation is completed, and tighten them as necessary.

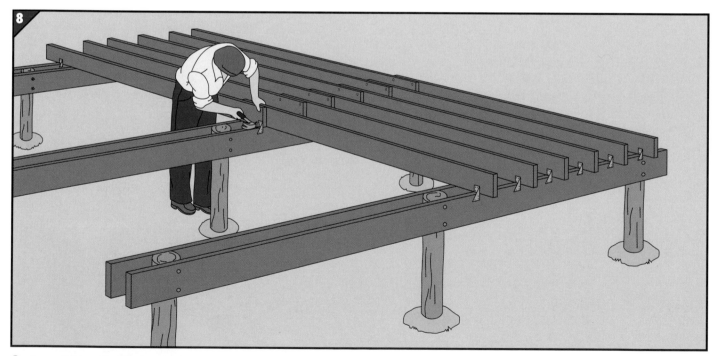

8. Attaching the floor joists.

◆ Set the joists across the beams at 16-inch intervals, letting them extend beyond the outside beams by a foot and overlap at the center beams by a foot.
◆ With 3-inch common nails, fasten together the joists that overlap at the center beams.
◆ Fasten the joists to the beams with multipurpose framing anchors and the nails recommended by the manufacturer of the anchors *(above)*.
◆ Nail header joists across the outside ends of the floor joists, and fasten them to the end of each joist with $2\frac{1}{2}$-inch common nails.
◆ Lay a subfloor across the joists *(page 33, Step 5)*.

Masonry Piers for Stronger Supports

Piers make a more durable foundation than wooden poles, and are almost as easy to put up. You can make them in three different ways: by pouring concrete into cylindrical fiber forms; by stacking and mortaring masonry-block piers and filling the cores of the blocks with concrete; or by setting precast piers of solid concrete.

Dealing with a Slope: As with pole platforms, piers can be used on gently sloping sites, provided the piers and their footing holes are deeper and wider than on a level site; consult a building professional. But if the slope is greater than 1 in 10—1 foot of rise in every 10 horizontal feet—you will have to build a continuous-wall foundation *(pages 24-28)*.

Footings: All three types of piers rest on footings—solid concrete bases that are wide and thick enough to support the structures above them. In general, a footing should be as thick as the width of a pier, and twice as wide—a pier 8 inches wide, for example, would require a footing 8 inches thick and 16 inches wide. Dig the holes so the bottom of the footing is 1 foot below ground, or 6 inches below the frost line, whichever is deeper.

Cast Cylinders: Fiber tubes 8 inches in diameter and 10 feet long make quick work of casting cylindrical concrete piers *(below and pages 21-22)*; store them upright and keep them perfectly dry until they are filled. Cylindrical piers can be built to any height, making it easy to set the tops of the piers to the same level.

Masonry Blocks: These blocks come in a wide range of sizes; single-core, 8- by- 12- by- 12-inch blocks make particularly sturdy piers *(page 23, top)*. Level the footings for block piers with a water level in the same way you level forms *(opposite, Step 3)*, but mark the height on the reinforcing bars (rebars), then measure down from the marks to set the height of the concrete for the footings.

Precast Piers: Although simple to install, these piers *(page 23, bottom)* are heavy and awkward to move and set into position. To level their footings, drive stakes into the footing holes, mark stakes with a water level as you would for concrete forms *(page 21)*, pour concrete up to the marks, and remove the stakes before the concrete begins to harden. Because they generally come no more than 18 inches high, they are used mainly on level sites that have a shallow frost line.

CASTING CONCRETE

1. Casting the footings.

◆ Locate and dig the footing-and-pier holes as for a pole platform *(page 16, Step 1)*, excavating each hole 16 inches wide to the required depth.

◆ At the center of each hole, drive a length of $\frac{1}{2}$-inch rebar into the ground until the top of the rod is about 6 inches lower than the planned height of the pier above ground *(right)*.

◆ Fill the first 8 inches of the holes with concrete, creating footings. Allow the concrete to cure for at least one day.

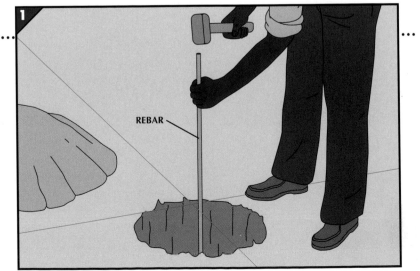

REBAR

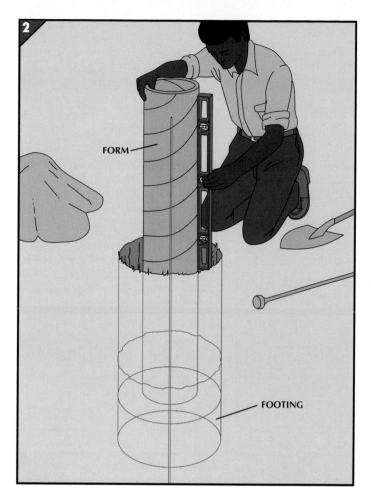

2. Positioning the forms.
◆ Slide a form over each rebar so it rests on the footing.
◆ Fill the hole around the form with earth, tamping it down firmly. After every 6 inches of fill, check that the form is vertical with a carpenter's level *(left)*.

FORM

FOOTING

CORNER FORM

3. Leveling the forms.
◆ Mark the planned height of the piers on a corner form.
◆ Have a helper hold one end of a water level or a transparent hose filled almost completely with water at the height of the mark on the corner form.
◆ Hold the other end against the next form in the row *(above)* and mark a line at the level of the water.
◆ Repeat the process to mark each form.
◆ Cut the forms at the marked heights with a hacksaw.

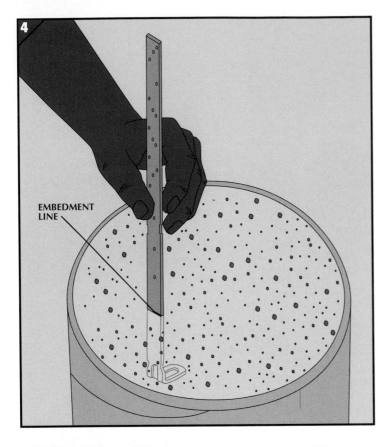

EMBEDMENT LINE

4. Embedding the anchors in concrete.

◆ With a helper and a string, go from form to form to align and mark the position of a beam anchor on the front and back of each form, ensuring that each beam—3 inches wide for doubled 2-by-10s or 2-by-12s, or $4\frac{1}{2}$ inches for a triple beam—will be centered on the pier.

◆ Mix enough concrete to fill the forms, then shovel it into each form in the row, using a length of rebar to pack the concrete down with every foot you add.

◆ As you fill each form, level the concrete off with the top of the form using a 2-by-4, then following the marks on the form, push an anchor that is as long as the width of the beams to be installed *(Step 5)* into the concrete down to the embedment line marked on it *(left)*.

◆ Embed anchors in concrete in the remaining forms in the same way.

◆ Double-check the alignment of the anchors with the string, adjusting them to line up as needed.

◆ Allow the concrete to cure for five to seven days.

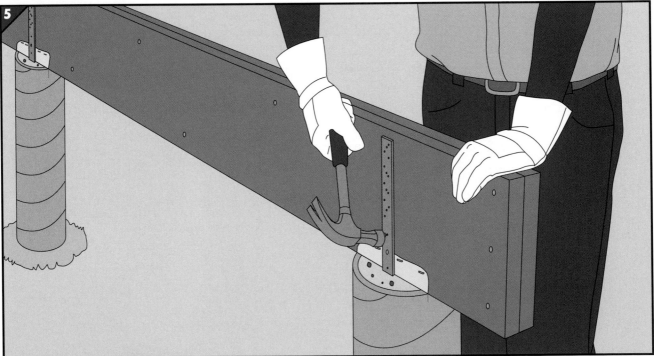

5. Attaching the beams.

◆ Make a beam for each row of piers: For a prefab cabin *(pages 36-43)*, nail pairs of 2-by-10s or 2-by-12s together with 3-inch galvanized common nails. Drive three nails in a row about 1 inch from each end and stagger nails along both edges at 10-inch intervals. For an A-frame *(pages 44-52)*, make triple beams.

◆ For a vapor barrier, set asphalt shingles on the piers, or cut 6-mil polyethylene sheeting into pieces to wrap around the bottom of the beam at each pier, and staple the pieces to the beam.

◆ Set the beam into its anchor, then check whether it is level. If not, shim the low end by placing galvanized washers between the beam and pier.

◆ Fasten the beam to each anchor by nailing into each hole *(above)*.

◆ Fasten joists to the beams as for a pole foundation *(page 19, Step 8)*, then lay a subfloor across the joists *(page 33, Step 5)*.

BLOCK AND PRECAST PIERS

Concrete-block piers.

◆ Cast a footing for each pier as for concrete piers *(page 20, Step 1)*, but level the footings by marking the rebars with a water level as for concrete forms *(page 21)*.

◆ To keep the heights of the piers consistent, make a story pole: On a piece of lumber, mark lines at intervals equal to the height of a block plus a $\frac{3}{8}$-inch mortar joint.

◆ Trowel a bed of mortar on the footing and lay a concrete block on the mortar, centering the block around the rebar.

◆ Add blocks and mortar to build up the pier, checking each course for level and plumb with a carpenter's level *(right)*, and for height with the story pole.

◆ Build each remaining pier in the same way, running a string between adjacent piers to keep them all consistent and in alignment.

◆ Fill the cores of the piers with grout—concrete thinned with water so it can be poured—then embed concrete anchors in the piers and attach beams as for concrete piers *(page 22, Steps 4 and 5)*

STORY POLE

FOOTING

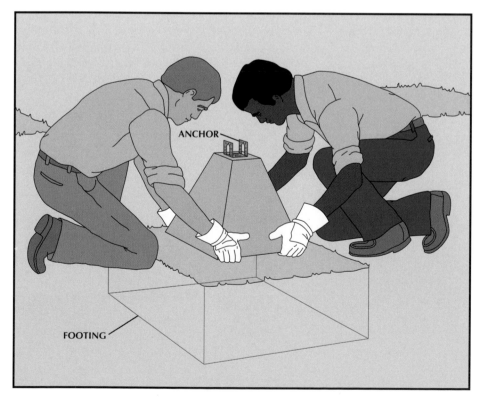

ANCHOR

FOOTING

Precast-concrete piers.

◆ Cast a footing for each pier as for concrete piers *(page 20, Step 1)*, but proceed immediately, before the concrete cures.

◆ With a helper, press a precast pier into the wet concrete *(left)*.

◆ With a carpenter's level, ensure that the pier is level.

◆ Position each remaining pier in the same way, running a string between adjacent ones to keep them aligned and level.

◆ Install vapor barriers and attach beams to the piers' built-in anchors as you would for concrete piers *(page 22, Step 5)*, nailing exterior-grade plywood spacers at 24-inch intervals between the boards making up the beam, if necessary, to ensure the beam sits snugly in the anchors.

A Continuous Block Wall

Foundations made of blocks resting on a footing of cast concrete are generally necessary in soil too unstable to support the pinpoint load of piers or poles, and in areas prone to earthquakes or hurricanes. If your cabin is in one of these areas *(pages 86-89 and 91-92)*, you will need to modify the techniques shown here. Heavy buildings such as log cabins also need this strong support. A wall foundation is easier to insulate as well, and allows plumbing to be housed in a crawl space—a must in areas with very cold winters. With some modifications, the design can be used on sites with slopes greater than 1 in 10 *(page 29)*.

Sizing the Foundation: Plan the job so the length of each foundation wall is a multiple of 8 inches—one-half the nominal length of a standard masonry block, plus a $\frac{3}{8}$- to $\frac{1}{2}$-inch mortar joint. Make the footings extend at least 12 inches below ground—or at least 6 inches below the frost line, whichever is deeper—and the walls rise 18 inches above ground. For deep footings—4 feet or more—have a professional excavate the trenches.

Materials: To determine the number of blocks you need, multiply the total length in feet of the walls by the number of rows—called courses—then by .75. The mortar can be made from 1 part Portland cement, 1 part hydrated lime, 6 parts damp sand, and water; or by combining 1 part premixed masonry cement, 3 parts sand, and water. For a large project, it is usually easiest to have the concrete delivered in a transit-mix and poured directly into the footing. If the truck cannot reach the footing, assemble a group of helpers with wheelbarrows and plywood chutes.

TOOLS

Maul	Water level	Mason's line
Hammer	Rebar cutter	Tin snips
Tape measure	Square-edged	Electric drill
(50-foot)	shovel	Circular saw
Plumb bob	Float	Carpenter's
Shovel	Chalk line	square
	Mason's trowel	Handsaw
	Level	

MATERIALS

1 x 2s, 1 x 6s	Galvanized common nails ($2\frac{1}{2}$", 3", $3\frac{1}{2}$")	Concrete blocks
2 x 4s, 2 x 6s	Rebar ($\frac{1}{2}$")	Metal mesh
2 x 8s, 2 x 10s	Rebar supports	Vents
Powdered chalk	Mechanic's wire (16 gauge)	Anchor bolts ($\frac{1}{2}$" x 8"), washers, nuts
Plywood ($\frac{3}{8}$")	Concrete mix	Grout
Exterior-grade plywood ($\frac{3}{4}$")	Polyethylene sheeting	Steel plates
Ring-shank nails ($2\frac{1}{2}$")	Mortar	Bricks

SAFETY TIPS

Goggles protect your eyes when you are bending rebar or hammering. Wear gloves, goggles, and a dust mask when mixing mortar and concrete. Hard-toed shoes prevent injuries from dropped blocks.

CASTING THE FOOTING

1. Locating the corners.
◆ Drive stakes at two adjacent corners of the planned foundation.
◆ Tack nails to the tops of the stakes and stretch a string between the nails.
◆ Drive a third stake along the line 3 feet from one corner and tack a nail to the stake.
◆ Have one helper hook a tape measure on the corner-stake nail and a second helper hook another tape measure on the stake at the 3-foot mark. Where the 4-foot mark on the first tape measure crosses the 5-foot mark on the second, drive a marker stake *(right)*. Use this marker and the corner stake to establish the

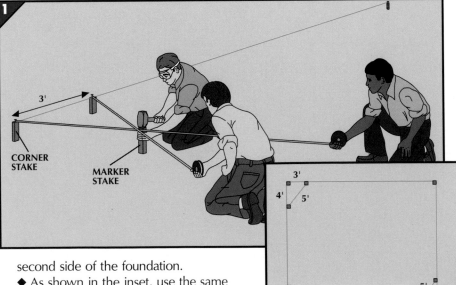

second side of the foundation.
◆ As shown in the inset, use the same method to mark the remaining two sides.

2. Positioning the walls.

◆ About 5 feet outside the corners of the planned foundation, set up four guides—called batter boards—each built from two 1-by-6s set at right angles and nailed to three 2-by-4 stakes.

◆ Stretch a string from a corner stake to the batter board at an adjacent corner and align it with the nail on the second corner stake, then mark the string's location on the batter board, defining the outside of the foundation wall *(right)*. Repeat the process to mark the outside foundation wall at each corner.

◆ As shown in the inset, make marks on the batter boards for the inside of the foundation wall and for the trench and footing: Place a mark $7\frac{5}{8}$ inches inside the first mark for the inside wall of the foundation. Mark the board 4 inches outside and 12 inches inside the first foundation mark to position the footing. For the trench,

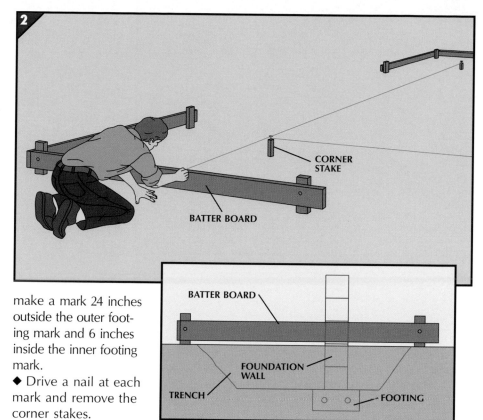

make a mark 24 inches outside the outer footing mark and 6 inches inside the inner footing mark.

◆ Drive a nail at each mark and remove the corner stakes.

3. Digging the trenches.

◆ Drive a 1-by-2 stake into the ground in line with each trench mark on the batter boards.

◆ Stretch strings between the stakes and trace the strings along the ground with chalk *(above)*.

◆ Dig the trenches 8 inches shallower than the footing depth.

◆ Stretch strings between the footing nails on the batter boards.

◆ Drop a plumb bob from the string to the bottom of the trench and mark lines for the footing with chalk.

◆ Dig the footing trenches 8 inches deeper than the trench.

4. Leveling the footing trench.

◆ Drive 1-by-2 stakes into the ground at each corner of the footing trench.
◆ Mark one stake 8 inches from the bottom of the trench.
◆ With a water level, transfer the mark to an adjacent corner stake *(left)*. Repeat for the three remaining corners.
◆ Drive a pair of stakes 3 inches from each side of the trench every 3 feet.
◆ Alternating from one side of the trench to the other, use the water level to transfer the 8-inch marks from the corner stakes to the intermediate stakes.
◆ Measure down from the mark on each stake to the bottom of the trench and deepen it to 8 inches where necessary.
◆ Make grade pegs by cutting $\frac{1}{2}$-inch rebar into 16-inch lengths, one for each stake, with a rented rebar cutter.
◆ Drive a peg into the trench next to each stake so the top of the peg is level with the mark on the stake.
◆ Remove the stakes, filling in the holes they leave with soil.

5. Casting a reinforced footing.

◆ Set lengths of $\frac{1}{2}$-inch rebar in the trench alongside each row of grade pegs, tying concrete rebar supports to the underside of the bars at 6-foot intervals to hold them 3 inches above the trench bottom. Metal rebar supports are also available *(photograph)*. Where two bars meet end to end, overlap them 12 inches. Cut bars to length if necessary with a rented rebar cutter.
◆ Where two pieces of the reinforcing rod meet, lash the bars together with 16-gauge mechanic's wire *(right)*.
◆ Pour concrete into the trench to just above the tops of the grade pegs, working it in with a square-edged shovel.
◆ Level and smooth the footing with a wooden float until the tops of the pegs and footing are at the same level. If specified in the local building code, pull out the grade pegs—use pliers—and fill the holes by chopping at the concrete with a gardening trowel, then refloat the surface.
◆ Cover the concrete with polyethylene sheeting and let it cure for seven days.

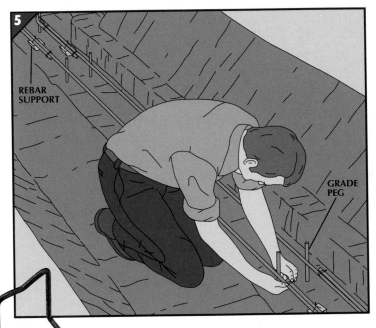

REBAR SUPPORT

GRADE PEG

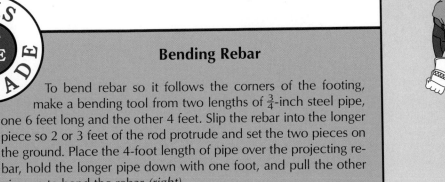

TRICKS OF THE TRADE

Bending Rebar

To bend rebar so it follows the corners of the footing, make a bending tool from two lengths of $\frac{3}{4}$-inch steel pipe, one 6 feet long and the other 4 feet. Slip the rebar into the longer piece so 2 or 3 feet of the rod protrude and set the two pieces on the ground. Place the 4-foot length of pipe over the projecting rebar, hold the longer pipe down with one foot, and pull the other pipe up to bend the rebar *(right)*.

BUILDING THE FOUNDATION WALL

1. Building the leads.

◆ Stretch strings between the outside-wall nails on the batter boards, drop a plumb bob from each line, and snap chalk lines on the footing.

◆ Make a dry run to ensure the blocks fit.

◆ Fashion a story pole (page 23, top) and spread a mortar bed 10 inches wide and $1\frac{1}{2}$ inches thick at one corner of the footing.

◆ Lay a corner block at the intersection of two chalk lines and tap the block down with a trowel until the mortar joint is $\frac{3}{8}$ inch thick.

◆ With a level, check that the block is level along its length and across its width.

◆ Lay four blocks on each side of the corner, making the mortar joints between blocks $\frac{3}{8}$ inch thick, and check that they are level.

◆ Set a corner block on top of the first one, and check the height of the blocks with the story pole (right).

◆ Repeat the procedure at the three remaining corners of the footing.

2. Leveling the first course.

◆ Hook a mason's line between two adjacent corner blocks level with the top of the first course of blocks.

◆ Finish laying the first course of blocks between the corners along the mason's line, adjusting the thickness of the mortar so the tops of the blocks are level with the line. If the wall will support the girder (page 31, Step 3), lay one solid block instead of a hollow-core one when you reach the middle. Fill in the first course between the remaining corners in the same way, laying a second solid block opposite the first one (left).

◆ Move the mason's line up and lay the second course of blocks, making sure that the two blocks resting on a solid block in the first course are also solid.

◆ Before spreading the mortar for the third course of blocks, use tin snips to cut a piece of metal mesh or hardware cloth two blocks long and 1 inch wider than the cores for every pair of blocks.

◆ Apply the mortar for the course and press the mesh into it, then lay the course. Center a solid block over each pair of solid blocks in the second course.

SOLID BLOCK

3. Venting the crawl space.

To provide adequate ventilation for the crawl space of your structure, install one vent in the wall for every 300 square feet of floor space. Locate vents in the fourth course of blocks, 4 feet from a corner. If you will be installing two vents, place them on opposite walls.

◆ As you lay the fourth course, omit one block for each vent, and make sure that the two blocks resting on a solid block in the third course are also solid ones. When the fourth course is in place, set the vent in the mortar *(right)* so it is inset 4 inches from the wall's outside face and the flanges on its top edge rest on the blocks to each side.

◆ Pack mortar around the edges of the vent, sloping the mortar downward at the bottom, to shed rain.

4. Forming girder pockets.

◆ Lay the fifth course like the third, but omit the mesh. Center two solid blocks over the vent and place a half block measuring 4- by 8- by 16 inches at the middle of the girder walls so it is flush with the outside face of the wall *(left)*, leaving a 4-inch shelf for the girder.

5. Setting anchor bolts.

For fastening the sill plate *(page 30, Step 1)*, you need to embed $\frac{1}{2}$- by-8-inch L-shaped anchor bolts in the blocks. Locate bolts 10 inches from each corner and every 20 inches along the walls in between. In a high-wind area, you can embed bolts for anchor-downs *(page 91, Step 1)* to reinforce the structure.

◆ Make a positioning jig for each bolt by drilling a $\frac{5}{8}$-inch hole through the middle of a 1-foot-long 2-by-6.

◆ Fill the cores of all the blocks with grout—concrete thinned with water so it can be poured—and trowel it flush with their tops.

◆ Slip an anchor bolt through its hole in a jig and thread a washer and nut onto the bolt about 1 inch from the threaded end. Position the jig on the wall flush with the outside faces of the blocks and tap the bolt into the grout so the washer is flat against the jig *(right)*.

◆ After 24 hours, remove the nuts, washers, and positioning jigs. Set the nuts and washers aside.

For sites with a slope greater than 1 in 10—1 vertical foot for every 10 horizontal feet—you will need to adapt the design of a continuous-wall foundation (pages 24-28). This can be done by casting a stepped footings for the walls that follow the slope (below). Because of local variations due to such factors as different soil types, have your plan checked by a building-code official in the

To make form boards for 8-inch-high steps, cut 2-by-8s to length and tack on strips of $\frac{1}{2}$-inch plywood cut $1\frac{1}{2}$ inches wide. Anchor them at the sides with stakes so the tops of the boards are level and 8 inches above the bottom of the trench. Fasten them together with $3\frac{1}{2}$-inch, easy-to-remove double-headed nails.

Cut $\frac{1}{2}$-inch rebar into lengths that can be bent to overlap at the middle of each step by at

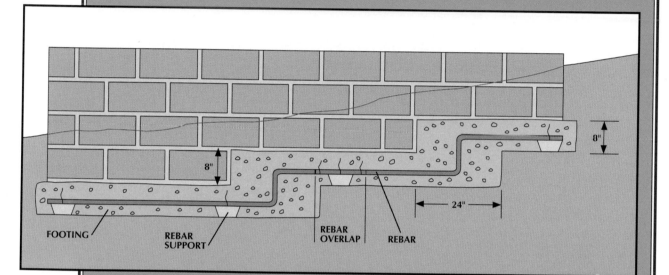

FOOTING   REBAR SUPPORT   REBAR OVERLAP   REBAR   8"   24"   8"

area, or a contractor familiar with local custom before you start to dig.

The walls at the top and bottom of the slope are built in the standard fashion, but the walls along the slope need stepped footing trenches. Dig the trenches so each step is a multiple of 8 inches deep. The number of steps you need depends on the difference in elevation between the high and low ends of the footing; a 4-foot difference on a mild slope, for example, would require five 8-inch steps. On a steeper slope the steps could be 16 or 24 inches.

To contain the concrete for the footing within the steps, build a series of wooden forms (right). Place the form boards for the front of the steps at least 24 inches—or the distance required by the building code or local custom—in front of the forward edge of the trench step.

least 12 inches, and anchor the rods with rebar supports and wire as on page 26, Step 5. When the concrete has cured, remove the form boards and stakes, and erect the block wall (pages 27-28).

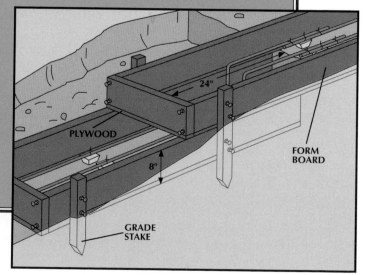

PLYWOOD   24"   FORM BOARD   8"   GRADE STAKE

FROM SILL PLATE TO GIRDER

1. Fastening the sill plate.

◆ Cut a 2-by-6 to the length of one foundation wall to make a sill plate.

◆ With a helper holding the plate against the anchor bolts on the wall so the ends are flush with the corners, use a carpenter's square to mark a line across the plate at the center of each anchor bolt (right).

◆ Measure the distance from the outside edge of the wall to the center of the bolt, transfer this point to each marked line, and drill a $\frac{3}{4}$-inch hole through the sill plate at each point.

◆ Slip the sill plate over the bolts and fasten it with the washers and nuts.

◆ Attach sill plates atop the three remaining walls in the same way, then toenail the ends of the boards together with 3-inch galvanized common nails.

◆ Above each girder pocket, cut a $1\frac{1}{2}$- by-$5\frac{3}{4}$-inch notch into the inside edge of the sill plate.

NOTCH

GIRDER POCKET

2. Locating the girder piers.

◆ Stretch a string between nails tacked into the sill plates above the center of each girder pocket.

◆ With a helper stretching a 50-foot tape measure along the string, hang rags from the tape to divide the distance between the nails into thirds (above).

◆ Drop a plumb bob from each rag and mark the ground for piers.

◆ Erect a masonry-block or cast-concrete pier at each location so its top is level with the bottoms of the girder pockets (page 23).

◆ Remove the nails and strings.

3. Making and placing the girder.

◆ Cut three 2-by-10s to fit between the notches in the sill plates, less 1 inch. Using the nailing pattern prescribed for doubled beams *(page 22, Step 5)*, form the boards into a girder by nailing them together *(right)*. If the span of the girder will exceed 16 feet, splice 2-by-10s end to end so the seams will sit on the piers.

◆ With a helper for every 5 feet of girder length, set the girder in its notches and on the piers, leaving $\frac{1}{2}$ inch of space between the ends of the girders and the backs of its notches.

◆ Check that the top of the girder is flush with the top of the sill plate; add steel plates or slate shims, if necessary.

◆ Fill empty spaces in the girder pocket with bricks cut in half. Leave $\frac{3}{8}$-inch mortar joints between the bricks and a $\frac{1}{2}$-inch gap on each side of the girder.

MASONRY-BLOCK PIER

GIRDER SPLICE

ADDING A FLOOR

1. Marking the sill plates for joists.

◆ Tack a nail into the sill plate $15\frac{1}{2}$ inches from the end of a long wall.

◆ Have a helper hook a tape measure on the nail, then mark joist locations on the sill plate at 16-inch intervals, drawing lines on both sides of the leg of a carpenter's square *(above)*.

◆ Repeat the marking procedure on the opposite-wall sill plate.

◆ Transfer the joist locations from the plates to the girder with a chalk line.

If you are building a log cabin *(pages 68-83)*, omit header and stringer joists. Once the sill logs are in place *(pages 69-72)*, install floor joists, a vapor barrier, and a subfloor *(pages 32-33, Steps 3-5)*.

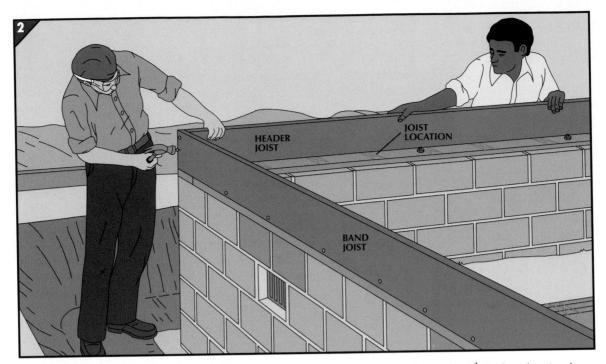

2. Nailing header and band joists.

◆ With a helper, set a 2-by-10 band joist on a marked sill plate, outside face flush with the outside of the wall, and toenail it to the plate with 2½-inch galvanized common nails.

◆ Position a 2-by-10 header joist on the adjacent sill plate, butt it against the band joist, and nail the joists together with 3½-inch galvanized nails (above).

◆ Fasten header and band joists together and to the remaining two plates in the same manner.

◆ With a carpenter's square, extend the joist-location lines from the sill plates to the inside faces of the header joists.

3. Filling in with joists.

◆ Measure and cut 2-by-10 joists to fit between one header joist and the middle of the girder.

◆ Set the first joist on the sill plate, aligned with its location marks, and nail it to the header joist.

◆ Toenail the joist to the girder.

◆ Fasten the first joist to the opposite header joist in the same way, then secure the seam between the joists by nailing a 9¼-inch square of ⅜-inch plywood to each side (above).

◆ Attach the next pair of joists in the same manner.

4. Laying a vapor barrier.

◆ Unroll a length of 3-foot-wide 6-mil polyethylene sheeting on the ground under the first two joists *(right)*.
◆ Weigh down the corners of the sheeting with brick or stones.
◆ Fasten two more joists *(page 32, Step 3)* and set down more sheeting, overlapping the first layer by 6 inches. Continue in this fashion until the last of the joists is fastened.

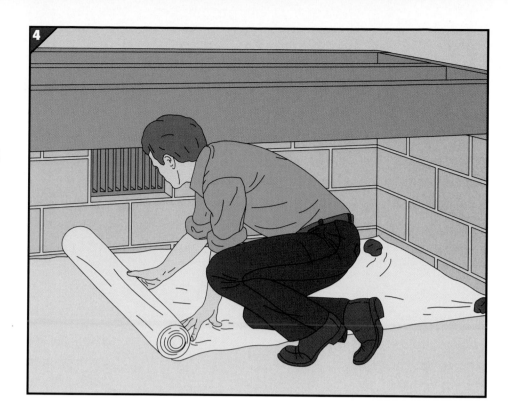

BLOCKING

5. Laying the subfloor.

◆ Cut 2-by-8s into 16-inch lengths of blocking.
◆ Nail the blocking between the joists at 4-foot intervals.
◆ Starting at one corner of the foundation, lay a $\frac{3}{4}$-inch exterior-grade plywood panel atop the joists—long edges perpendicular to the joists.
◆ Fasten the panel to the joists and blocking with $2\frac{1}{2}$-inch ring-shank nails spaced 6 inches apart around its perimeter, and 12 inches along the joists *(left)*.
◆ Nail down the rest of the floor in the same way, leaving a $\frac{1}{8}$-inch gap all around each panel. Stagger the end joints between rows of panels—cutting the first sheets of each row in half if necessary.

Four Simple Structures

Esthetic preferences or personal lifestyles may be guiding factors when you are deciding on a cabin design. Whether you want a sophisticated chalet or a rustic retreat, you can begin with one of the four basic structures shown on the following pages. All can be built by an amateur with a minimum of special skills and tools, and each can suit a particular taste or solve a special construction problem.

Trimming a joist →

A Cottage of Prefab Panels

The vacation house most like a year-round home has standard stud walls covered with siding *(below)*. An advantage to this structure is that its walls can be prefabricated in sections, hauled to the site in a small truck and, with three or four helpers, quickly assembled on the floor of the cabin and topped with a simple rafter or truss roof *(pages 56-63)*.

Planning: To ensure that the sections fit together properly, draw a scaled plan of the structure before building the panels. Indicate the size of the foundation and the location and dimensions of walls, doors, and windows. You can simplify construction by ordering doors and windows that fit between studs *(opposite)*. If you are planning to build your cabin with a shed

roof *(pages 56-57)*, you'll need to make the back wall higher than the front, or one side wall higher than the other.

Wall Panels: The wall frames are built in multiples of 4 feet—a size that suits common building materials. The economical cabin shown on these pages uses 8-foot exterior siding, and has ceilings just under 7 feet high. If you want higher ceilings, cut the wall studs longer and buy 10-foot siding—which costs a bit more—and trim it to length.

Place the assembled panels on the truck in order so that the last one you load is the first to be erected; this way, you can unload and assemble the walls in sequence.

If you are building the cabin in an area prone to earthquakes *(pages 86-89)* or hurricanes *(pages 91-92)*, you will need to modify some of the techniques shown in this section.

TOOLS	MATERIALS			SAFETY TIPS
Sawhorses	1 x 3s, 1 x 4s,	Common nails (2", 3", $3\frac{1}{2}$")	Wood screws (2" No. 6)	*Goggles protect eyes from injury when you are using power tools or hammering.*
Screwdriver	1 x 6s	Galvanized common and box nails (2")	Hinges	
Circular saw	2 x 2s, 2 x 4s,		Exterior plywood siding ($\frac{5}{8}$")	
Electric drill	2 x 6s	Galvanized finishing nails ($2\frac{1}{4}$")	Aluminum flashing (6")	
Saber saw	Plywood ($\frac{1}{2}$")			
Hammer				
Tin snips				
Cold chisel				
Carpenter's square				
Carpenter's level				
Maul				
Chalk line				

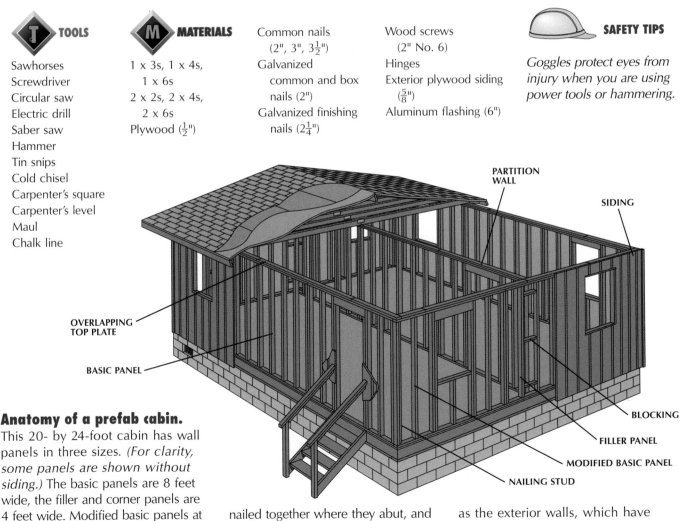

Anatomy of a prefab cabin.

This 20- by 24-foot cabin has wall panels in three sizes. *(For clarity, some panels are shown without siding.)* The basic panels are 8 feet wide, the filler and corner panels are 4 feet wide. Modified basic panels at each corner provide a nailing surface for the end stud of the adjoining corner panel. The wall sections are nailed together where they abut, and connected by an overlapping top plate, installed on site. Interior partition walls are framed the same way as the exterior walls, which have blocking where the partitions adjoin them. Any foundation *(pages 15-33)* or roof *(pages 64-67)* can be used.

The basic panel.

Each panel is made from seven 2-by-4 studs cut 6 feet 9 inches long. The 2-by-4 top and soleplates are cut 8 feet long, and the studs are fastened to the plates at 16-inch intervals with the middle stud in the center of the panel so wallboard and interior paneling can be nailed there. Two pieces of $\frac{5}{8}$-inch vertical siding are nailed to the studs and plates flush with the outside faces of the outer studs so they project above the top plate by $1\frac{1}{2}$ inches and below the soleplate by $10\frac{1}{2}$ inches.

Filler panels are made in the same way, but with four studs and one piece of siding, so they are only 4 feet wide. A basic panel can be adapted to accommodate a window or door as shown for the modified and corner panels below.

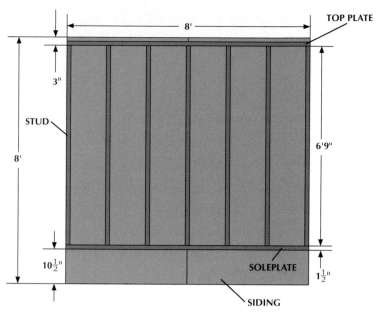

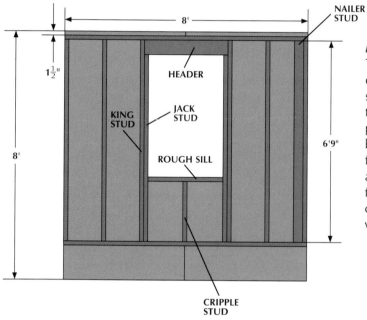

A modified basic panel.

To tie walls together at a corner, an extra "nailer" stud is added—flush with the inside edge of the soleplate—at the left end of a basic panel—when viewed from the outside—to serve as a nailing surface for the first stud of the adjoining corner panel. For a panel with a window opening, a header, made with $\frac{1}{2}$-inch plywood nailed between two 2-by-6s, spans the top of the opening; jack studs nailed to the king studs at either side of the opening support the header; a rough sill is toenailed to the jack studs; and a cripple stud braces the rough sill.

A corner panel.

The top and soleplates of this panel are 7 feet $8\frac{1}{2}$ inches long, with the stud at the corner spaced only $12\frac{1}{2}$ inches from the next stud. The sheathing overlaps the corner end by $3\frac{1}{2}$ inches. When the panel is put in place, the overlapped siding attaches to the end stud of a modified basic panel. Because the siding always overlaps to the right when viewed from outside, erect the walls from left to right. A door opening is framed much like that of a window, but the rough sill and cripple stud are omitted.

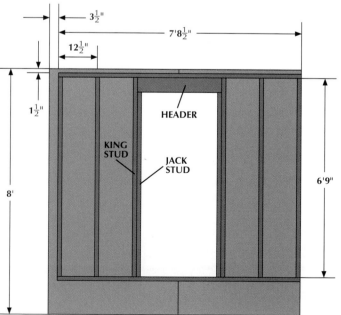

1. Sizing the studs with a jig.

◆ To make a jig that will enable you to cut several studs to length in a single operation, secure a plywood panel atop a pair of sawhorses with 2-inch common nails. With 3-inch nails, attach a 2-by-4 stop along one side of the panel, and a 2-by-2 stop along an end, perpendicular to the side stop. With a hinge, fasten a 2-by-2 guide at a 90-degree angle across the side stop and panel; locate the guide so that the studs will be the correct length when you run a circular saw along it.

◆ Swing the saw guide up and put the 2-by-4s edge to edge in the jig so they are butted against the end stop and the first board is flush against the side stop. Lower the guide in place.

◆ Holding the 2-by-4s steady, run a circular saw across the boards with the base plate against the guide (above).

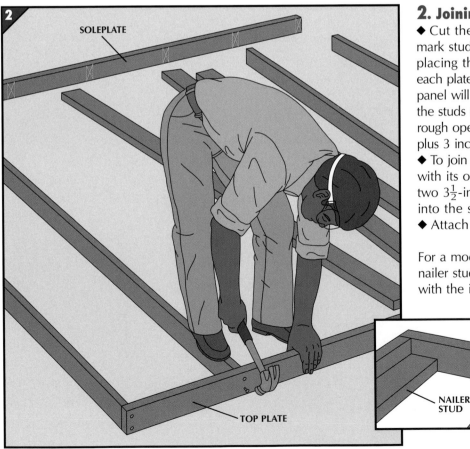

2. Joining the studs and plates.

◆ Cut the top and soleplates to length, then mark stud locations on one face of each board, placing the middle-stud mark in the center of each plate and the rest at 16-inch intervals. If the panel will have a window or door opening, space the studs on each side of the gap according to the rough opening required for the window or door, plus 3 inches.

◆ To join the studs and top plate, align the stud with its outline, stand on the board, and drive two $3\frac{1}{2}$-inch common nails through the plate into the stud (left).

◆ Attach the soleplate the same way.

For a modified panel (page 37, middle), add a nailer stud butted against the last stud and flush with the inside of the top and soleplates (inset).

For a corner panel (page 37, bottom), locate the last stud at the corner $12\frac{1}{2}$ inches from the next one.

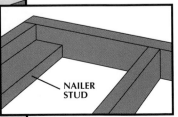

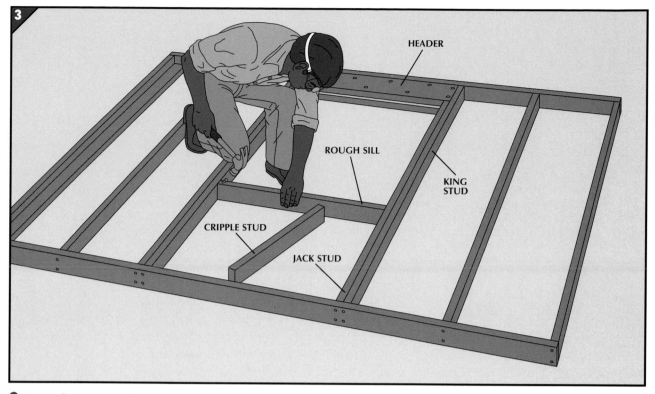

3. Framing a rough opening for a window.

◆ To make the header, first cut two 2-by-6s and a $\frac{1}{2}$-inch plywood spacer of the same width to fit in the opening; sandwich the spacer between the 2-by-6s and secure the assembly with $3\frac{1}{2}$-inch common nails driven every 10 inches in a staggered pattern.

◆ Cut two jack studs to fit between the header and soleplate, and fasten them to the king studs at each side of the opening.

◆ Cut a 2-by-4 rough sill to fit between the jack studs and fasten it *(above)*, spacing it from the header the distance indicated by the window manufacturer's specifications.

◆ Cut a 2-by-4 cripple stud to fit between the sill and soleplate, then nail it to both boards.

Frame a door opening in the same way, but omit the sill and cripple stud.

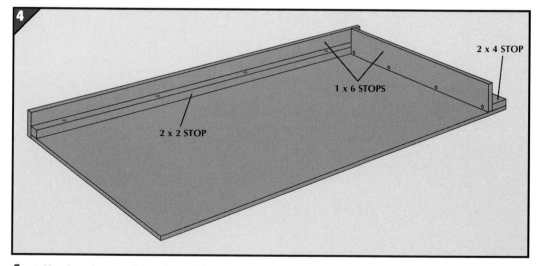

4. A jig for fastening the siding.

◆ Cut a 2-by-2 stop 8 feet long and nail it along one edge of a plywood panel.

◆ Cut a 2-by-4 stop 3 feet $10\frac{1}{2}$ inches long and fasten it along an end of the panel.

◆ Cut two 1-by-6s to the lengths of the two stops; then, with 2-inch No. 6 wood screws, fasten one to the inside edge of the 2-by-4 and the other to the outside of the 2-by-2.

5. Adding siding to basic panels.

◆ Set the siding jig on the floor and place the panel on it so the top plate rests flush against the 2-by-2 stop and an outer stud sits against the shorter 1-by-6 stop.

◆ Place a sheet of $\frac{5}{8}$-inch exterior siding atop the panel so one end and edge are butted against the 1-by-6 inch stops.

◆ With $2\frac{1}{2}$-inch galvanized box nails, fasten the siding to the top and soleplates and studs, leaving $\frac{1}{8}$ inch between panels and driving the fasteners at 6-inch intervals around the perimeter and every 12 inches along the studs *(above)*.

If the panel has a window or door opening, turn it over and drill a hole through the sheathing at each corner of the opening. Join the holes with pencil lines and cut the siding along the marks with a saber saw.

6. Covering end panels.

◆ Modify the jig by moving the shorter 1-by-6 from the inside to the outside of the 2-by-4 stop *(inset)*.

◆ Nail the siding to the frame *(right)*.

7. Flashing an opening.

◆ With tin snips, cut a piece of 6-inch aluminum flashing to the width of the rough opening.

◆ Bend the aluminum over a 2-by-4 to a 90-degree angle, forming two flanges.

◆ Loosen the siding around the header with a cold chisel or pry bar.

◆ Slip one flange of the flashing between the header and the paneling *(left)*, then nail the flashing and siding to the header.

ERECTING THE PANELS

1. Bracing the first panel.

◆ Have two helpers hold a modified basic panel plumb at one end of the foundation, positioning the nailer stud at the corner.

◆ With 3½-inch common nails, attach a 2-by-4 brace to the second stud, fasten a short board to the bottom of the brace, and nail the board to the subfloor *(right)*.

◆ Fasten a brace at the other end of the panel to hold it plumb.

◆ Anchor the panel to the foundation by nailing its soleplate to the subfloor, driving a nail through the plate between each pair of studs.

NAILER STUD

BRACE

2. Extending the wall.
◆ Position the second panel against the first.
◆ With a helper holding the panel upright, use a 4-pound maul to align it with the first *(above)*.
◆ Plumb and brace the second panel, then nail the abutting joists of the two panels together.
◆ Repeat the process to raise three of the four walls, working from left to right (when viewed from outside the cabin) so each corner has a modified panel and an overlapping corner panel.
◆ Bring the interior walls inside, then raise the fourth wall.
◆ With 2-inch galvanized nails, fasten the sheathing of the corner panels to the nailer studs of the modified panels.

3. Tying the walls together.
◆ Cut a 2-by-4 top plate 4 feet long and, with $3\frac{1}{2}$-inch nails, fasten it atop the top plate of a corner panel so it overlaps the top plate of a modified panel *(right)*.
◆ Continue in this fashion around the perimeter of the wall, nailing on 8-foot-long plates that overlap the seams between adjacent panels. Cut the last 2-by-4 of each wall to fit against the adjoining wall.
◆ Working outside, cover the exposed edges of the siding with 1-by-3s and 1-by-4s fastened with $2\frac{1}{4}$-inch galvanized finishing nails. Nail on the 1-by-4 first so it overlaps the corner by $\frac{3}{4}$ inch, then attach the 1-by-3 flush against the 1-by-4.

MODIFIED PANEL

OVERLAPPING TOP PLATE

CORNER PANEL

RAISING PARTITIONS

1. Locating the wall.

◆ With a helper at each side wall, snap a chalk line across the subfloor at one side of the proposed wall. To locate a wall directly above the girder, measure the distance between one foundation wall and the girder from below the floor, then transfer the measurement to the floor.

◆ Snap a parallel line $3\frac{1}{2}$ inches from the first *(right)*.

2. Erecting the wall.

◆ Cut six 2-by-4 blocks to fit between the studs on each side of the chalk lines on the subfloor.

◆ With $3\frac{1}{2}$-inch common nails, fasten three pieces of blocking to each wall, one near the bottom, one at the middle, and one near the top *(left)*.

◆ Raise the interior wall as you did the exterior ones *(pages 41-42, Steps 1-2)*.

◆ Fasten the outer studs of the first and last interior-wall panels to the blocking.

◆ Nail together the end studs of the wall panels, then tie the panels together *(page 42, Step 3)*.

The A-Frame: A String of Sturdy Triangles

One of the sturdiest of all structures is the A-frame, whose skeleton consists simply of a row of triangles. The bases of the triangles are the joists that support the floor, and the sides are the rafters that hold the combined walls and roof. The simplicity of construction and comparatively low cost make it a popular choice for vacation cabins. Any style of foundation *(pages 15-33)* can serve as its base.

Planning the Structure: The most common shape is equilateral—joists and rafters are equal in length and set at angles of 60 degrees to each other; however, you can use different angles to modify the shape *(chart, below)*. An A-frame can be built to almost any size simply by varying the number of triangles and their dimensions, but a cabin with a sleeping loft must have rafters at least 20 feet long to allow adequate headroom on both floors. For a small structure like the one on these pages, three people can lift the assembled triangles into place without the assistance of special equipment; a structure with rafters greater than 24 feet may prove too unwieldy for a crew

of amateurs. Frame doors and windows in the end walls; for a large A-frame, plan a lot of windows to keep the interior from being too dark.

Finishing Touches: If the A-frame includes a loft *(page 50)*, provide it with stairs or a ladder, and a sturdy railing. Rest a deck, if you build one, on the same foundation as the main structure and surround it with a railing *(pages 51-52)*. Buy deck stairs at a building center or construct them on site. Install insulation between the floor joists, rafters, and end-wall studs as you build.

 TOOLS

Screwdriver
Circular saw
C-clamps
Electric drill
Hammer
Carpenter's level
Carpenter's square
Plumb bob
Wrench
Saber saw

 **MATERIALS**

1 x 2s, 2 x 4s
2 x 6s, 2 x 8s
Pressure-treated
  2 x 6s, 2 x 10s,
  4 x 4s
Exterior-grade
  plywood ($\frac{3}{4}$")
Wood glue

Common nails
  (2", $2\frac{1}{2}$", $3\frac{1}{2}$")
Galvanized
  common nails
  ($2\frac{1}{2}$", 3", $3\frac{1}{2}$")
Ring-shank nails
  ($2\frac{1}{2}$")
Wood screws
  ($1\frac{3}{4}$" No. 8)
Roofing materials

Carriage bolts
  ($\frac{5}{8}$" x 6";
  $\frac{1}{2}$" x 4", 6")
Lag screws
  ($\frac{1}{2}$" x 4")
Multipurpose and
  framing anchors
  and nails
Wooden ladder
Concrete mix

 **SAFETY TIPS**

Protect your eyes with goggles when using power tools or hammering. Wear gloves when handling pressure-treated lumber; add a dust mask when cutting it.

COMMON FLOOR-TO-RAFTER ANGLES

Rafter Length	Joist Length	Rafter/Joist Angle	Rafter/Rafter Angle
16'	12'	68°	22°
16'	14'	64.1°	26°
16'	16'	60°	30°
20'	12'	72.5°	17.5°
20'	14'	69.5°	20.5°
20'	16'	66.4°	23.6°
20'	20'	60°	30°

Anatomy of an A-frame.

This 20-foot-per-side equilateral A-frame rests on tripled 2-by-10 pressure-treated beams supported by masonry-block piers *(page 23)*. The triangles, spaced 24 inches apart, are formed of 2-by-8 rafters joined at the apexes with plywood gussets and sandwiched at the bottom by pairs of pressure-treated 2-by-6 joists. (A cabin larger than this structure would require correspondingly larger framing lumber.) At the end walls and under the sleeping loft, horizontal 2-by-6 collar beams are fastened between the rafters. The rafters of the end walls are doubled to provide a flush nailing surface for the exterior sheathing. The sleeping loft, reached by a ladder, is framed by a railing secured to posts and rafters. Knee walls along the sides of the cabin provide concealed storage areas. The deck rests on 2-by-6 joists set 16 inches apart. Posts for the railing are secured to the deck joists; the stairs are set on concrete footings and are attached to the deck with metal framing anchors. All exposed wood is pressure-treated lumber. Although an asphalt-shingle roof is shown, any of the roofing alternatives in this book *(pages 64-67)* could be installed.

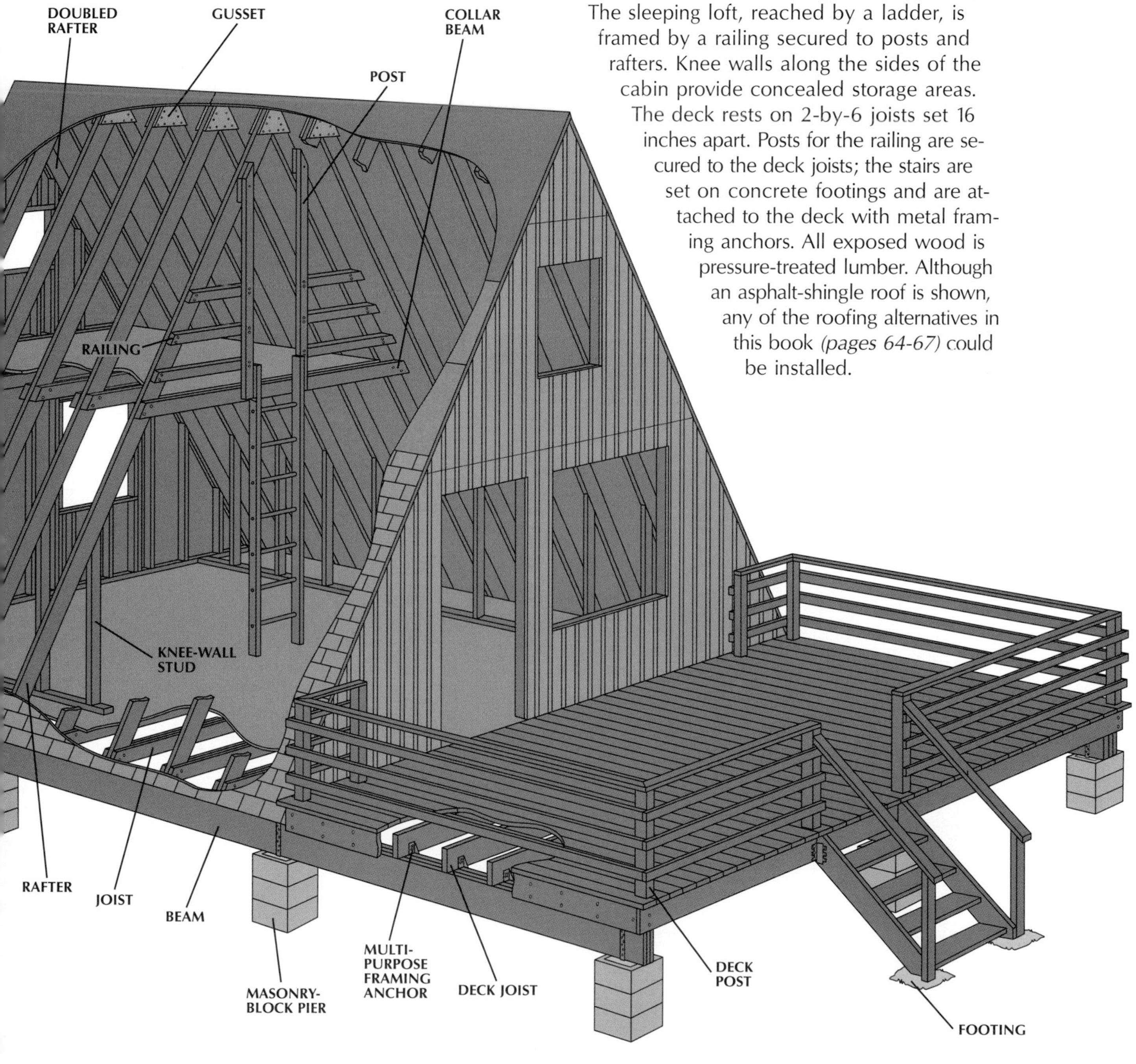

DOUBLED RAFTER
GUSSET
COLLAR BEAM
POST
RAILING
KNEE-WALL STUD
RAFTER
JOIST
BEAM
MASONRY-BLOCK PIER
MULTI-PURPOSE FRAMING ANCHOR
DECK JOIST
DECK POST
FOOTING

1. Cutting joists and rafters.

To cut the joists and rafters quickly, make a jig for each angle to be cut.

◆ Mark a scrap board at the angle of the joists or rafters *(page 44, chart)* and set it on a work surface.

◆ Place a 2-by-4 on each side of the board and fasten them down with screws.

◆ Align a 1-by-2 with the mark and screw it to the 2-by-4s as a cutting guide.

◆ Run a circular saw along the guide, cutting a kerf through all three boards.

◆ Remove the scrap board and replace it with a joist or rafter, marked to length. Align the mark with the kerf and cut the board *(right)*. Cut the other end so both cuts angle toward the middle.

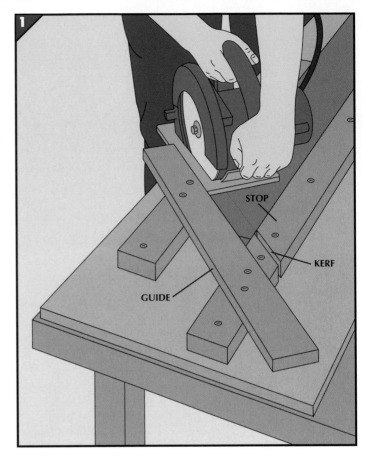

EASY ANGLES WITH A MITER SAW

A power miter saw can cut joists and rafters to the appropriate angles without the need of a jig. The model shown at left features a radial arm that allows the blade to slide back and forth for wide stock. Simply swivel the base of the saw to the desired angle and lock it in place. Hold the board against the base and fence with the blade. Keeping your hand safely away from the blade, squeeze the trigger, and lower the blade over the board. For big jobs, set the saw on sawhorses or a couple of concrete blocks.

FENCE

BASE

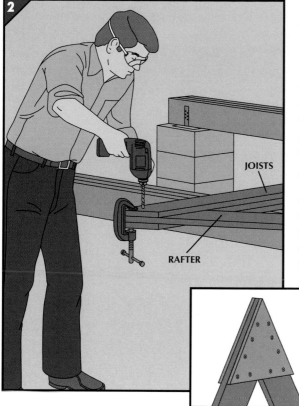

2. Assembling the triangles.

◆ Clamp the ends of two joists around the base of a rafter, aligning the ends and edges of the boards, and drill a $\frac{5}{8}$-inch hole through the three layers (*left*).
◆ Fasten the boards together with a $\frac{5}{8}$- by 6-inch carriage bolt, washer, and nut.
◆ Bolt the opposite ends of the joists to the base of another rafter in the same way.
◆ From $\frac{3}{4}$-inch exterior grade plywood, cut two triangular gussets to the same angle as the A-frame.
◆ Butt the top ends of the rafters together and fasten the gussets to each side of the seam with wood glue and $1\frac{3}{4}$-inch No. 8 wood screws (*inset*).
◆ Add a second carriage bolt to each joist-rafter joint.
◆ Assemble the remaining triangles in the same way, but secure gussets to just one side of each end triangle.
◆ Allowing for at least 7 feet of headroom, mark both rafters of each triangle at the end walls and under the loft for collar beams. For each triangle, cut two collar beams (*opposite, Step 1*) to fit between the outside edges of the rafters, then bolt them on as you did the joists.
◆ Cut 1-by-2 spacers to the joist width and fasten them with 2-inch common nails between all the pairs of joists and collar beams at 2-foot intervals.
◆ Double the rafters of the end triangles: Cut four lengths of rafter lumber—two to fit between the joists and collar and two between the beams and rafter peaks—and nail them to the outsides of the rafters with $2\frac{1}{2}$-inch nails.

3. Erecting the triangles.

◆ Mark the triangle locations on the beams at 2-foot intervals.
◆ Nail scabs—1-foot-long 2-by-4s—to the insides of the outer beams on each side of the marks for the front end triangle.
◆ With a pair of helpers, lift and position the end triangle on the beam between the scabs.
◆ Plumb the triangle and brace it with two 2-by-4s nailed diagonally between the rafters and outer beams so the top of each brace is least $4\frac{1}{2}$ feet from the base of the rafters.
◆ Position and plumb the remaining triangles in the same way, bracing them with a 1-by-2 nailed to each side of the adjacent triangle (*right*).
◆ When all the triangles are braced, remove the scabs and attach the triangles to the beams, installing a multipurpose framing anchor to each side of every joist. In a high-wind area, use hurricane ties (*page 92*). Nail the bottom corners of the triangles to the beams.
◆ Sheathe the outside of the frame, laying decking for shakes (*pages 66-67*), or 4-by-8 panels of $\frac{5}{8}$-inch exterior-grade plywood for metal roofing (*page 64-65*) or asphalt shingles (*page 66*). Work from bottom to top, fastening the sheathing with $2\frac{1}{2}$-inch common nails. Leave a $\frac{1}{8}$-inch gap around panels and stagger the joints. Remove the bracing after you lay the bottom course of panels.
◆ Cover the floor with plywood (*page 33, Step 5*).

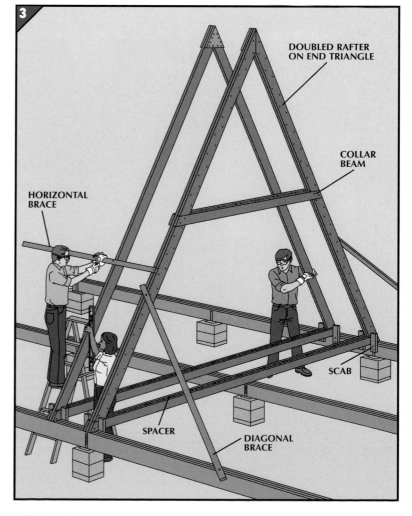

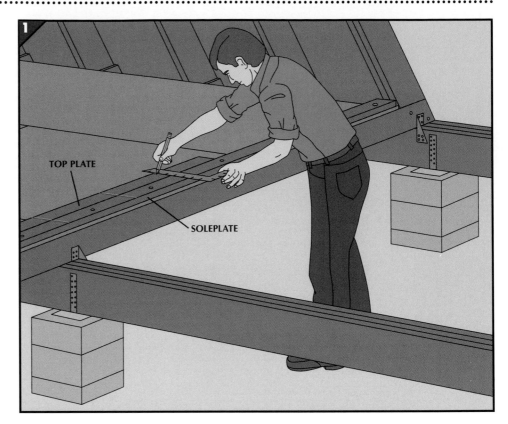

1. Making the plates.

◆ Cut a 2-by-4 soleplate to fit between the rafters at each end of the floor, and fasten them in place with 2½-inch common nails spaced 16 inches apart.

◆ Cut a top plate to fit under the collar beam directly above each soleplate.

◆ Set a top plate against its sole-plate, centered between the longer board's ends, and use a carpenter's square to mark a stud location every 16 inches across both boards *(right)*. Mark the other top plate in the same way.

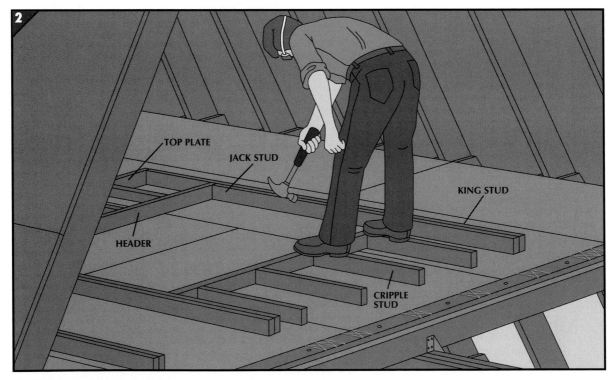

2. Raising the end walls.

◆ Cut studs to fit between the top and soleplates and toenail them to the top plate, framing doors or windows *(above)* as for a prefabricated frame cottage *(page 37)*, but using 2-by-4s for headers and fastening cripple studs between the headers and top plates.

◆ With helpers, tilt each wall upright and set the studs on their marks on the soleplate.

◆ Keeping the wall plumb with a carpenter's level, toenail each stud to the soleplate with 3-inch nails and fasten the top plate to the underside of its collar beam.

3. Attaching the mitered studs.

◆ Set a 2-by-4 on the floor against the soleplate.

◆ Stand a 2-by-4 stud on the board in line with one of the unoccupied stud marks, hold it plumb, and mark a line across its face along the bottom edge of the rafters *(left)*.

◆ Cut the stud to length and toenail it to the rafters and the soleplate.

◆ Frame the remaining portions of the walls above and below the collar beams in the same way.

◆ Sheathe the outside of the end walls with $\frac{3}{4}$-inch exterior-grade plywood.

PUTTING IN KNEE WALLS

Framing the walls.

◆ Cut two 2-by-4 soleplates to fit between the end-wall plates and position one along each side wall at a distance that will create a useful storage area behind the knee wall without cutting off too much floor space.

◆ Hang a plumb bob from each rafter in turn and mark the soleplate for studs.

◆ Mark and miter a stud as described in Step 3 above, then use it as a template to trim the remaining studs.

◆ Fasten the studs to the soleplate with $3\frac{1}{2}$-inch common nails, tilt the frame into position, and nail the plate to the floor and the studs to the rafters with $2\frac{1}{2}$-inch nails *(left)*.

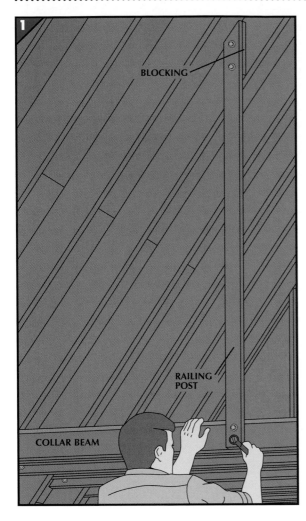

1. Bolting railing posts.

◆ In the loft, mark locations for 2-by-4 posts on the outside face of the front collar beam to either side of the place you plan to put the ladder.

◆ Cut the posts to fit between the bottom of the beam and the top of the rafters directly above.

◆ Cut 2-by-4 blocking to fit between each post and rafter.

◆ Clamp the post to the beam, drill a $\frac{3}{8}$-inch hole through the post and into the beam, and attach the post with a $\frac{1}{2}$- by-4-inch lag screw.

◆ Plumb the post, drill through the post, blocking, and rafter, and secure the assembly with two $\frac{1}{2}$-by-6-inch carriage bolts.

◆ Add a second lag screw to the bottom of each post (left).

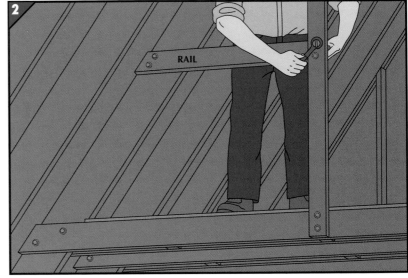

2. Attaching the railing.

◆ Cut a 2-by-4 railing to span between the outside edges of each post and rafter 3 feet above the loft floor; miter one end of the board to match the roof slope.

◆ Fasten the railing to the back of the railing post and to the front of the rafter with two $\frac{1}{2}$- by-6-inch carriage bolts at each location (above).

◆ Add two more rails to each post spaced no more than 6 inches apart.

◆ Fasten a wooden ladder to the collar beam with framing anchors.

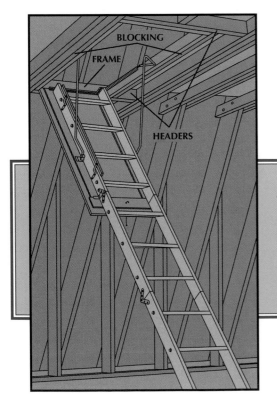

A FOLDING LADDER TO THE LOFT

To save floor space downstairs, install a folding ladder to access the loft. For the model shown at left, frame an opening in the loft floor by fastening headers between adjacent collar beams and adding blocking between the headers; use collar beam-size lumber for the headers and blocking. Attach the ladder, which comes mounted to a frame, to the framing according to the manufacturer's instructions.

1. Laying the understructure.

◆ With multipurpose framing anchors, fasten a 2-by-6 deck joist cut as long as the cabin's width across the beams, flush against the outer joist of the first triangle. If the width exceeds 20 feet, splice two shorter joists over the middle girder.

◆ Attach a joist every 16 inches until you reach the beams' ends.

◆ Cut two 2-by-6 perimeter boards to fit against the ends of the deck joists. Attach the boards along the sides of the deck with $3\frac{1}{2}$-inch galvanized common nails *(left)*; fasten their inside faces to the joists with framing anchors.

2. Installing railing posts.

◆ Set a $3\frac{1}{2}$-foot-long pressure-treated 4-by-4 post on the beam at each corner of the deck and clamp it securely.

◆ Drill a hole through the perimeter board into each post and two holes through the deck joist for $\frac{1}{2}$-by-4-inch carriage bolts and fasten the post in place *(right)*.

◆ Bolt two posts to the inside of the outer deck joist on either side of the stairway opening, resting one post on the middle beam, if possible. Brace the posts by nailing 2-by-6 blocking between adjacent joists and bolting the posts to the blocking.

◆ With 3-inch galvanized common nails or No. 8 wood screws, fasten 2-by-6 decking boards spaced $\frac{1}{4}$ inch apart across the joists; notch the decking, as necessary, to fit around the railing posts.

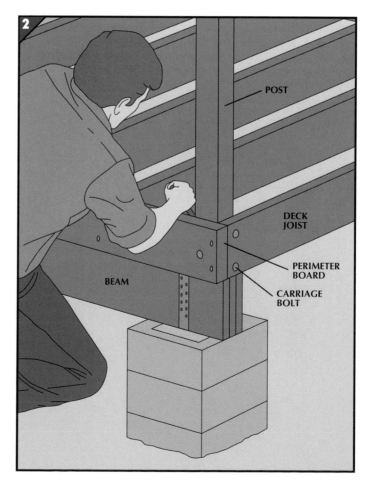

3. Completing the rail.

◆ Cut 2-by-4 rails to fit along the outsides of adjacent posts.

◆ With $2\frac{1}{2}$-inch galvanized common nails, fasten bottom rails to the outside faces of the posts at the distance from the decking specified by local code—typically no more than 4 to 6 inches.

◆ Attach two sets of middle rails and a top rail to the posts at the same intervals, mitering the ends of the top rails that meet over the posts.

◆ To enclose the corners of the deck at the end wall, first screw 3-foot-long rails to each corner post and nail them to studs in the end wall. Then, cut a notch in the decking with a saber saw to accommodate a 4-by-4 post and bolt the post to the joist. Add a top rail and toenail the post to the bottom and middle rails (right).

4. Mounting stairs.

◆ Pour a concrete footing to support the bottom of each stair stringer—the diagonal board that runs along the sides of the steps.

◆ Fasten the tops of the stringers to the outer deck joists with framing anchors (left).

◆ Bolt a 4-by-4 bottom post to the outside of each stringer with two $\frac{1}{2}$-by-6-inch carriage bolts so the post rests on the footing.

◆ Cut 2-by-4 handrails to fit between the bottom posts and the deck posts 2 inches below the top rails.

◆ With $3\frac{1}{2}$-inch galvanized nails, fasten the handrails to the posts parallel with the stringers.

A House Suspended on Poles

Building a pole-frame cabin is not much different from erecting a pole-platform foundation *(pages 15-19)*. In each case, pressure-treated poles are anchored in the ground and horizontal beams are bolted to them to support an understructure that serves as both foundation and floor. The pole-frame cabin requires longer poles on the sides to support additional beams for the roof, and the outer beams on the outside poles are omitted. The resulting structure is a rustic but sturdy vacation home that has even greater resistance to storms and floods than one that simply rests on a platform.

Building the Understructure:
A one-story cabin is built around two outside rows of 15-foot poles and one or more middle rows of 6- to 7-foot poles, all sunk and secured like those of a pole platform *(page 16)*, and spaced no more than 8 feet apart. For a shed roof *(pages 56-57)*, taller poles are needed on one side. For a structure up to 16 feet wide *(below)*, one middle row is needed and single 16-foot 2-by-10s serve as support beams. For a wider or longer

cabin requiring additional poles, use shorter joists or beams and overlap them at the intermediate poles. Rent metal scaffolding *(page 62)* to install the eave beams, and work with at least two helpers to set the heavy and cumbersome outside poles.

Bracing and Aligning the Poles:
After you have set the poles in the ground, the techniques of bracing and aligning them vary only slightly from those used for the pole platform. Plumb the inner surfaces of the side poles by placing a long straight board against the pole and a 4-foot level on the board. As you plumb each pole, brace it two-thirds of the way up. When you cut daps in the outside poles for floor beams *(page 17)*, you will have to complete the recesses with a wood chisel. Cutting daps for the eave beams can be handled entirely with a saw. Once these supports are in place, the cabin is ready to be walled *(pages 36-43)* and roofed *(pages 64-67)*. When raising the walls, trim corner panels to fit against the middle poles and caulk the seams between the panels and the poles.

 TOOLS

Power auger	Bucksaw
Shovel	Wood chisel
Posthole digger	Mallet
Carpenter's level	Combination
Circular saw	square
Hammer	Electric drill
2 x 4 tamper	Auger bit ($\frac{1}{2}$")
	Wrench

 **MATERIALS**

1 x 2s	Ring-shank nails
Pressure-treated	($2\frac{1}{2}$")
poles (6"-8"	Carriage bolts ($\frac{1}{2}$"),
thick), 2 x 6s,	washers, nuts
2 x 8s, 2 x 10s	Multipurpose
Exterior-grade	framing anchors
plywood ($\frac{3}{4}$")	and nails
Common nails	Concrete mix
($1\frac{1}{2}$", 3")	Siding and roofing
	materials

 **SAFETY TIPS**

Goggles protect your eyes when you are hammering and using power tools. Wear gloves when handling pressure-treated lumber; add a dust mask when cutting it.

Anatomy of a pole-suspended cabin.
Two outside rows of tall poles and a middle row of short ones support and frame this cabin. Double 2-by-10 floor beams set in notches called daps are bolted to each row of middle poles to support the floor joists, whose ends rest on single outer floor beams; 2-by-6 blocking nailed between the floor joists every 4 feet stabilizes the understructure and provides a nailing surface for plywood subflooring. Double 2-by-8 eave beams set in daps and bolted to the outside poles support the roof framing. Stud walls sheathed with wood panels close in the walls. This roof is covered with asphalt shingles, but any roofing material described on pages 64 to 67 can be laid down. A prefabricated set of steps completes the exterior of the structure.

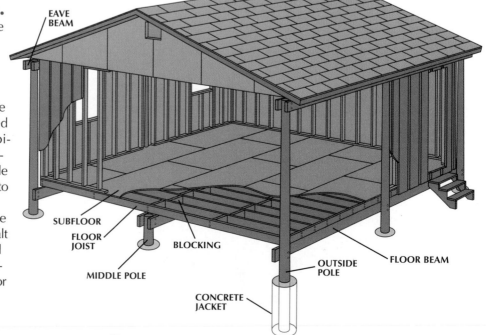

EAVE BEAM

SUBFLOOR

FLOOR JOIST

BLOCKING

MIDDLE POLE

OUTSIDE POLE

FLOOR BEAM

CONCRETE JACKET

1. Putting up the poles.
◆ Dig holes for all the poles *(page 16, Step 1)*.
◆ Cut a 2-by-10 about 10 inches longer than the depth of the holes.
◆ To help guide a long outside pole into its hole, place the 2-by-10 in the hole, then, with two helpers, brace one end of the pole against the board and tilt it up until the pole drops into the hole.
◆ Set all the outside poles in their holes in the same way *(right)*, then lower the short middle poles into their holes.
◆ Align all the poles and set them in concrete *(page 16, Step 2)*.

2. Attaching the floor beams.
◆ Start daps on the inner sides of the poles with a bucksaw *(page 17, Step 3)*, then clean out the cuts with a wood chisel.
◆ Nail a pressure-treated 2-by-10 floor beam in the daps in each row of poles *(page 18, Step 5)*.
◆ With a combination square, measure from the beam along both sides of each middle pole, marking a dap on the outside that will be of uniform depth and parallel to the one on the inner side.
◆ Cut the dap, then make the remaining ones in the same way, marking all those in the row to a consistent depth *(left)*.
◆ Nail the outer beam to the middle poles with a 3-inch nail, then bolt all the beams in place *(page 19, Step 7)*.

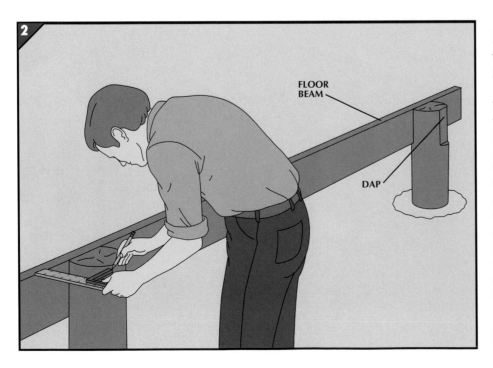

3. Installing joists and subfloor.

◆ Cut pressure-treated 2-by-6 joists to span across the beams, then lay them down *(page 19, Step 8)*, tying the joists to the beams with multipurpose framing anchors *(right)*. Along each side wall, nail the header joist to the ends of the floor joists in two sections, butting its inside ends against the middle pole.

◆ Cut enough 2-by-6 blocking to fit between adjacent joists at 4-foot intervals, and fasten it to the joists with 3-inch common nails.

◆ Nail a plywood subfloor to the joists *(page 33, Step 5)*.

4. Fastening the eave beams.

◆ With a helper, measure up 8 feet from the subfloor and mark a dap on the inner side of each pole for a double 2-by-8 eave beam *(left)*.

◆ Cut the daps.

◆ Bolt the beams to the poles in the same way as you did for the floor beams.

◆ Cut the tops of the poles flush with the upper edges of the eave beams.

◆ Install siding *(pages 36-43)*, sizing the wall sections to rest flush against the middle poles. Seal the seams between the siding and poles with caulk.

◆ Frame the roof *(pages 56-63)*.

A Strong Framed Roof

A basic roof frame of rafters in either shed or gable style makes an appropriate topping for a prefab frame cottage *(pages 36-43)* or one suspended on poles *(pages 53-55)*.

A Shed Roof: For this style of roof, each rafter extends over the whole width of the building. To make one side wall higher than the other, modify some of the techniques prescribed for building a basic structure. For the prefabricated frame cottage, use longer studs and two tiers of panels to build the higher wall. For the pole-supported cabin, install taller poles on the high side.

Gable Roofing: Rising from both walls to a central ridge beam, a gable roof *(pages 58-60)* permits the use of

lighter and less expensive rafter stock than the shed roof *(chart, below)*.

Roof Slope: Before choosing and cutting the rafters—and before deciding on the height of the taller wall of a shed roof—decide on the slope of the roof. While a roof with a gentle slope is lighter and faster to build, areas subject to heavy snowfalls may require a steep pitch *(page 96)*. Slope depends on the roofing material; metal roofs *(pages 64-65)* can have a gentler slope than roofs covered with asphalt shingles *(page 66)* or wood shakes *(pages 66-67)*.

Siding: Install Z-flashing to seal the horizontal seams between siding panels of high shed-roof walls, or between the gables and walls of any cabin.

TOOLS
Chalk line
Hammer
Carpenter's level
Circular saw
Handsaw

MATERIALS
1 x 2s, 1 x 4s, 1 x 6s
2 x 4s, 2 x 8
Rafter and joist lumber
Plywood panels
Exterior plywood siding ($\frac{5}{8}$")

Common nails (2", 3", $3\frac{1}{2}$")
Galvanized box nails ($2\frac{1}{2}$")
Multipurpose framing anchors and nails
Roof sheathing
Roofing materials

SAFETY TIPS

Protect your eyes with goggles when you are hammering and using power tools.

Choosing rafters.

Refer to the chart at right when choosing the size of rafter stock. It provides the maximum span—the distance between the tops of the two side walls of a shed roof, or the ridge beam and one side wall of a gable roof—for five board sizes, depending on whether you space the rafters 16 or 24 inches apart. If the cabin is in an area that experiences heavy snow, you will need larger lumber *(page 96)*.

Rafter Spacing	16"	24"
Board Size	**Maximum Span**	**Maximum Span**
2 x 4	5'	N/A
2 x 6	9'	$6\frac{1}{2}$'
2 x 8	11'	$9\frac{1}{2}$'
2 x 10	14'	12'
2 x 12	18'	$15\frac{1}{2}$'

FRAMING A SHED ROOF

1. Marking the bird's-mouth cuts.

◆ Snap a chalk line down the middle of a rafter board and hold the board against the end of the building so that the chalk line touches the top plates of the high and low walls.
◆ Tack the board to the plates.
◆ At the low end of the board, outline the top plate and outside of the wall *(right)*. At the high end, mark the top plate and inside of the wall.

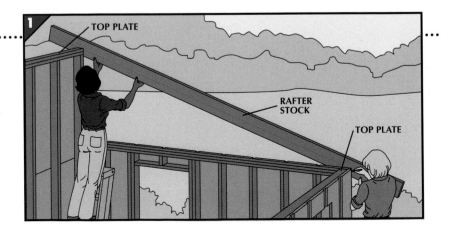

TOP PLATE

RAFTER STOCK

TOP PLATE

2. Marking the overhang cuts.

◆ Have your helper use a carpenter's level to mark a vertical line across the rafter board 12 to 18 inches from the wall or at the point you have chosen for the overhang *(right)*. Mark the same overhang at the high end of the rafter.

◆ Cut each rafter end at the vertical lines, then cut the rafters along the plate outlines for the bird's-mouth notch.

END RAFTER

MULTIPURPOSE FRAMING ANCHOR

3. Attaching the rafters.

◆ Mark rafter locations at 16- or 24-inch intervals *(chart, opposite)* on the top plates of the two walls.

◆ Set a multipurpose framing anchor on the top plate at each mark so the anchor's vertical flange is flush with the inside edge of the outline, then nail each one in place.

◆ Fit a rafter over the marks at one end of the structure and nail it to the framing anchor. In a high-wind area, use hurricane ties *(page 92)*.

◆ Fasten the remaining rafters in the same way *(left)*.

4. Installing gable studs.

◆ In line with each stud of the gable walls, mark a location for a 2-by-4 gable stud.

◆ Hold a 2-by-4 even with the first outline, with the wide face flat against the outsides of the wall and end rafter. Using a carpenter's level to keep the board vertical, mark it along the top plate and the bottom edge of the rafter across it *(right)*. Mark the remaining gable studs in the same way.

◆ Cut the 2-by-4s to length and toenail them to the top plate and rafter with $3\frac{1}{2}$-inch common nails.

◆ Finish the gable ends by fastening $\frac{5}{8}$-inch exterior plywood siding to the gable studs with $2\frac{1}{2}$-inch galvanized box nails *(page 40, Step 5)*.

◆ Sheathe the rafters as you would for an A-frame *(page 47, Step 3)*, and lay down the roof *(pages 64-67)*.

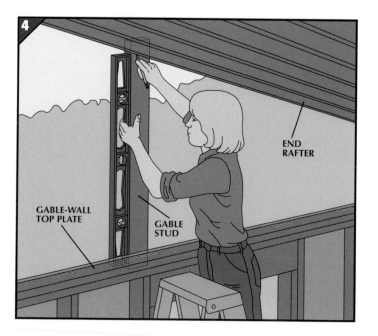

GABLE-WALL TOP PLATE

GABLE STUD

END RAFTER

CONSTRUCTING A GABLE ROOF

1. Installing joists.

◆ Mark ceiling joist locations on the side-wall top plates at the same interval you will use for the rafters (page 56).

◆ For each pair of marks, cut a joist to span between the outer edges of the side-wall top plates.

◆ With multipurpose framing anchors, fasten the first joist to the top plates $1\frac{1}{2}$ inches from the gable wall, locating the anchors on the inside faces of the joist.

◆ Attach the rest of the joists in the same way, but place the anchors on the opposite side of the joists (right). Fasten the last joist at the opposite gable wall in the same way as the first.

If the joists will cross over a load-bearing partition wall (page 43), you can use lumber half as long as the width of the cabin. Butt the joists end to end over the center of the wall's top plate and secure the seams with metal braces called gussets (inset).

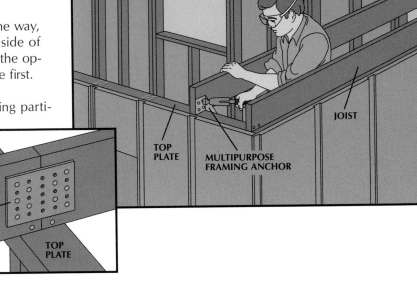

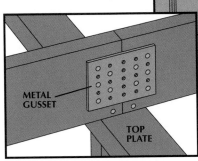

METAL GUSSET

TOP PLATE

TOP PLATE

MULTIPURPOSE FRAMING ANCHOR

JOIST

RIDGE-BEAM SUPPORT

2. Nailing ridge-beam supports.

◆ For each gable wall, cut a 1-by-6 the height of the roof peak as measured from the top plate of the end wall. Nail to it a pair of 1-by-2s cut 14 inches long, extending $7\frac{1}{2}$ inches above the top of the 1-by-6 and spaced $1\frac{1}{2}$ inches apart, forming a ridge-beam support.

◆ With 2-inch common nails, fasten the supports to the insides of the end joists so the tops of the 1-by-2s are at the height of the roof peak (left).

◆ Brace each support with a 1-by-4 nailed to the joist.

3. Placing the ridge beam.

◆ Place plywood panels on the ceiling joists to create a temporary floor for working on the roof frame.

◆ Cut a 2-by-8 ridge beam the length of the cabin and mark the rafter positions on both sides of the ridge beam according to rafter spacing appropriate for your cabin *(page 56)*.

◆ With a helper, raise the ridge beam to the scaffolding and cradle it in its supports *(right)*.

4. Preparing the rafters.

◆ Mark the first rafter *(page 79, Step 1)*, drawing a miter cut at the ridge beam *(left)* and a bird's-mouth notch at the top plate.

◆ Cut all the rafters to length *(page 79, Step 2)*.

5. Nailing the rafters.

◆ With one helper keeping the outermost rafter against the mark on the ridge beam, and a second helper holding the other end on the top plate and against the joist, fasten the rafter to the ridge beam with 3-inch common nails *(left)*. In a high-wind area, use hurricane ties *(page 92)*.

◆ Have the helper at the lower end of the rafter nail the rafter to the joist.

◆ Attach the opposite rafter in the same way, but toenail it to the ridge beam.

◆ Repeat the procedure to install the pair of rafters at the other end of the structure.

◆ Fasten the remaining rafters, but attach each rafter to the top plate with a multi-purpose framing anchor before nailing it to the joist.

6. Trimming the joists.

◆ With a circular saw, trim the protruding corners of the joists flush with the top edges of the rafters, using the rafter as a guide for the saw blade *(right)*.

◆ Remove the ridge beam supports, attach gable studs, and sheathe the gable ends as you would for a shed roof *(page 57, Step 4)*.

◆ Sheathe the rafters as for an A-frame *(page 47, Step 3)*, then lay down the roof *(pages 64-67)*.

Ready-Made Roof Framing

The simplest way to build a gable roof is with factory-made trusses *(box, below)*, eliminating the time-consuming job of cutting and fastening rafters. To make the work easier and safer, rent two adjustable scaffolds to position and fasten the units.

Ordering Trusses: A truss manufacturer or distributor can suggest the style of truss that is most suitable for your project. The design you choose is dictated by load—including probable snow load—roof span, and slope. The roof slope—generally at least 4 inches of vertical rise for every foot of horizontal run—needs to be appropriate for the climate and the type of roofing material you will use *(pages 56 and 64-67)*. When ordering trusses, specify the size of the desired overhang at the eaves and the dimensions of the vent openings in the end trusses.

 TOOLS

Tape measure
Hammer

Circular saw
Saber saw
Scaffolds
Carpenter's level

 MATERIALS

Stakes
1 x 6s, 2 x 4s
Exterior-grade
  plywood siding
  ($\frac{5}{8}$")

Trusses
Common nails
  ($2\frac{1}{2}$", 3")
Galvanized com-
  mon nails ($3\frac{1}{2}$")
Galvanized box
  nails ($2\frac{1}{2}$")

Multipurpose
  framing anchors
  and nails
Roof sheathing
Roofing materials

 **SAFETY TIPS**

Wear goggles when driving nails, and put on a hard hat for overhead work.

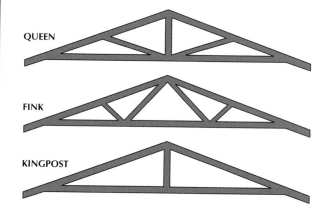

QUEEN

FINK

KINGPOST

A TRUSS FOR EVERY PURPOSE

Trusses are made of 2-by-4s fastened into triangles with metal gussets. The sides of the triangle—called the top chords—take the place of rafters, while the base—or bottom chord—serves as a ceiling joist. Diagonal webs connect the top and bottom chords, transferring the weight of the roof to the walls of the structure.

The combination of diagonal and vertical webs in the Howe style of truss *(photograph)* provides increased strength in an area with heavy snowfall. The Queen—essentially a Howe truss without vertical webs—is the most common design, while the Fink—with no center web—allows a catwalk storage space above the bottom chords. The Kingpost is the simplest of all, but as it has only a center web, it needs larger or higher-grade lumber to achieve the proper strength. A standard KIngpost is generally recommended for short and medium spans. End trusses *(page 62, Step 3)* have vertical webs to accommodate siding and a vent opening.

HOWE

TOP CHORD

WEB

BOTTOM CHORD

GUSSET

ERECTING A SET OF TRUSSES

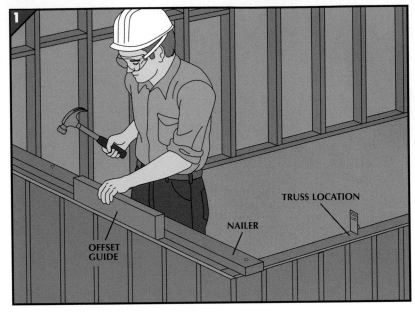

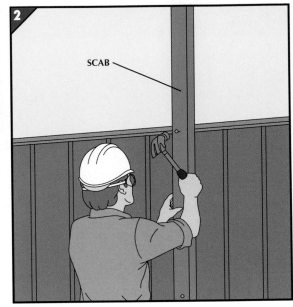

1. Preparing the walls.

◆ Along the top plates of the front and back walls—or the eave beams of a pole-frame cabin—mark a truss location every 24 inches.
◆ At each mark, fasten a multipurpose framing anchor.
◆ To provide nailing surfaces on the gable walls for the end trusses, cut 2-by-4 nailers to span between the outer edges of the front and back top plates—or eave beams.
◆ With 3-inch common nails spaced 24 inches apart, fasten a nailer to the top plate of each gable wall, offsetting it $1\frac{1}{2}$ inches from the outside edge with a 2-by-4 guide *(above)*.

2. Putting up temporary scabs.

Nail a 2-by-4 scab to a gable-wall stud about one-third of the way in from each corner so the board extends 4 feet above the nailer on the top plate *(above)*.

For a pole-frame cabin—where the roof is framed before the walls—position the scabs at the corners, and extend them from the ground to 4 feet above the eaves.

3. Raising the end trusses.

◆ Fasten $\frac{5}{8}$-inch exterior-plywood siding to each end truss, then cut a vent opening in the siding *(page 40, Step 5)* and frame it.
◆ With two helpers on scaffolds, set an end truss upside down on top of the front and back walls. Wedge a 2-by-4 into the peak of the truss and push it upright *(left)*.
◆ Walk the truss to the gable wall and have the helpers position it between the nailer and scabs.
◆ With $3\frac{1}{2}$-inch galvanized common nails, fasten the top chords to the scabs and the bottom ones to the nailer.
◆ Install the other end truss in the same way.

BRACE

4. Plumbing the trusses.

◆ Loosen the scabs from one of the end trusses and nail a long 2-by-4 brace diagonally to the vent framing.
◆ After you plumb the truss with a carpenter's level *(left)*, have a helper nail the brace to a stake in the ground.
◆ Plumb the opposite end truss in the same way.

5. Bracing the trusses.

◆ Cut several 1-by-6s to brace the trusses as you install them, and mark truss locations on them.
◆ Raise a standard truss and nail it to the first pair of framing anchors on the front and back walls.
◆ With 2½-inch common nails, fasten the end of a bracing board to the top chord of the end truss. In a high-wind area, use hurricane ties *(page 92)*.
◆ Nail the standard truss to the brace so the truss aligns with its location mark *(right)*.
◆ Nail a second brace across the top of the trusses on the opposite side of the ridge.
◆ Install and brace the remaining trusses in the same way, adding bracing boards as necessary.
◆ Sheathe the trusses as you would for an A-frame *(page 47, Step 3)*, fastening the roof sheathing to the trusses' top chords and removing the braces as you go.
◆ Nail braces across the tops of the bottom chords. In a high-wind area, add 1-by-6 diagonal braces between the webs of each end truss and the bottom chord of the fifth truss from each end truss.
◆ Remove the scabs and install the roofing material *(pages 64-67)*.

BRACING BOARD

Covering the Roof

Many cabins, like most houses, are roofed with asphalt shingles, but two somewhat less common materials may be more appropriate for your cabin or cottage: metal roofing and wooden shakes.

Metal Roofing: Metal roofing is economical and fire resistant, and for areas subject to heavy snowfalls, it provides a slippery surface that sheds snow before it can build up. Metal panels can be applied to a roof with a pitch of at least 3 inches of vertical rise for every 12 inches of horizontal run. The metal roofing shown here can be purchased in kits, which are available at most farm-equipment and building-supply dealers. The roofing comes in a variety of colors, with panels cut to specified lengths and with specially formed trim pieces or flashings to fit at the eaves, rakes, and ridge. Use a screw gun or drill to drive the appropriate fasteners at the intervals indicated by the manufacturer. The location of sealing strips and the correct overhang of the panels at rakes and eaves will also be indicated.

Shingles and Cedar Shakes: Available at home centers or lumberyards, asphalt shingles, wood shingles, and cedar shakes require at least a 4-in-12 slope. Shakes (*pages 66-67*), though expensive, provide the most rustic covering. The methods illustrated on the following pages, simplified from those prescribed for year-round homes, are suitable for vacation and weekend cottages in moderate climates. A starter course of smooth-surfaced shingles is laid along the eaves, and the rest of the roof is covered with rough hand-split shakes.

Shakes are laid on an open deck of 1-by-4s spaced at an interval that is $\frac{1}{2}$ inch less than one-half the length of the shakes.

TOOLS
Electric drill
Screwdriver bit
Tin snips
Hammer
Utility knife
Shingler's hatchet

MATERIALS
1 x 4s
Common nails ($2\frac{1}{2}$")
Roofing nails ($1\frac{1}{4}$")
Hot-dipped galvanized box nails ($1\frac{1}{2}$", 2", 3")
Roofing felt (15- or 30-pound)
Metal-roofing kit
Asphalt shingles
Cedar shakes and shingles

SAFETY TIPS
Goggles protect your eyes when you are driving nails. When working with metal roofing, wear work gloves to protect your hands. Put on nonslip rubber-soled shoes before you climb onto the roof.

SNOW-SHEDDING METAL

1. Installing the rake panels.
◆ Starting at the eaves, attach 30-pound roofing felt with $1\frac{1}{4}$-inch roofing nails, overlapping sheets by 6 inches.
◆ At the eaves, attach the eave drip edge included in the roofing kit with the fasteners provided (*inset*).
◆ Lay a sealing strip on the eave drip edge, parallel to the eave, then place the first metal panel with its end overhanging the eave so it is square to the eave and rake (*left*).
◆ Attach the panel by driving the fasteners supplied through the sealing strip and into the roof. Then fasten the panel along its length, staggering screws along each side at 1- to 2-foot intervals.
◆ Continue installing panels along the rake in the same way until you reach the ridge.

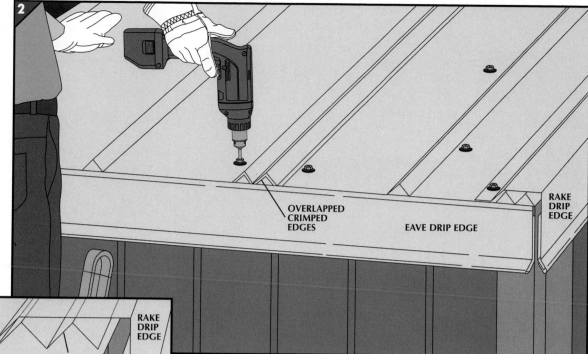

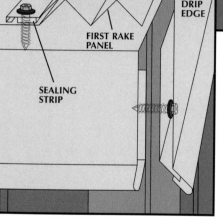

2. Covering the rest of the roof.

◆ Lay a sealing strip parallel to the rake over the first rake panel, then place the rake drip edge over the strip and fasten it through the eave drip edge and sealing strip *(inset)*.

◆ To install the other panels, place each one with its crimped edge overlapping the crimped edge on the adjacent panel, and with the overhang of the panels at the eaves equal to that of the first rake panel. Fasten the panels to the roof *(above)*. If you need more than a single panel length to extend from the eave to the ridge, overlap successive pieces by 3 to 6 feet, installing sealing strips at their ends.

◆ At the opposite rake, cut the last panels with tin snips, if necessary. Install them, then add the sealing strip and rake drip edge along the rake.

◆ Cover the other side of the roof in the same way.

3. Attaching the ridge cover.

On each side of the ridge, lay a sealing strip parallel to the ridge, then position a ridge cover over the ridge and attach it to the roof by driving the screws through the sealing strips *(right)*.

AN ASPHALT-SHINGLE ROOF

Laying courses of shingles.

◆ Install roofing felt as for a metal roof (page 64, Step 1), but lay 15-pound felt.

◆ For the starter course, cut the three tabs off the shingles with a utility knife and remove 6 inches from the first shingle.

◆ With four $1\frac{1}{4}$-inch roofing nails per shingle, fasten the starter course so the shingles overhang the eaves and rakes by $\frac{1}{4}$ inch. In each shingle, drive four nails below the line of adhesive (inset): one nail above each cutout and one nail 1 inch from each end.

◆ Fasten two shingles of the first course over the starter course.

◆ For the second course, cut half a tab from the first shingle on the end that will abut the rake, nail it down, then attach the second shingle. Install two shingles in the third, fourth, and fifth courses in the same way, starting each one with a shingle cut half a tab shorter than the course below to create a stepped pattern on the roof.

◆ Lay the sixth course by nailing a half-tab to the roof, then adding a full

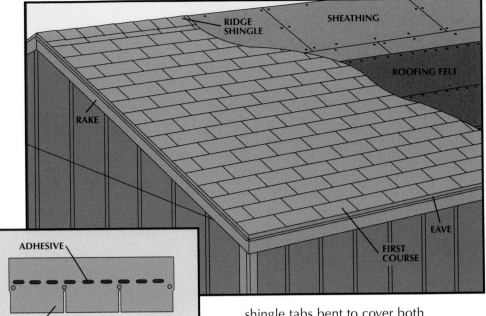

shingle. At the seventh course, repeat the pattern used for the first six courses. When you reach the rake, return to the eaves and add two-full size shingles to each course. Continue the process to cover the roof; trim the last course of shingles even with the ridge.

◆ Finish the ridge with individual

shingle tabs bent to cover both sides, starting with a tab at each end of the roof $\frac{1}{4}$ inch beyond the rakes; working toward the middle, overlap succeeding tabs by 7 inches. Trim the top end of the last tab so at least 5 inches of the tab it covers is exposed. Bend a half tab in two and nail it over the two tabs that overlap at the middle of the ridge.

LAYING DOWN SHAKES

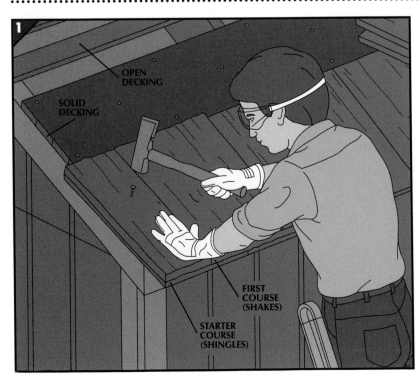

1. Laying a double starter course.

◆ For the first 3 feet up from the eave, install solid decking—1-by-4s fastened edge to edge to the rafters with $2\frac{1}{2}$-inch common nails. Continue up to the ridge laying open decking (page 64). At the ridge butt the last two rows of decking boards together.

◆ Cover the solid decking with 30-pound roofing felt, securing it with $1\frac{1}{4}$-inch roofing nails.

◆ With $1\frac{1}{2}$-inch hot-dipped galvanized box nails, fasten a starter course of cedar shingles, overhanging the eave by 2 inches and the rakes by $1\frac{1}{2}$ inches.

◆ Nail an 18-inch-wide strip of roofing felt over the shingles, 10 inches above the eave.

◆ Driving 2-inch box nails with a shingler's hatchet, lay the first course of shakes over the shingles, aligning the ends, but offsetting vertical joints by at least $1\frac{1}{2}$ inches (left).

2. Laying the remaining courses.

◆ Cut a scrap shake to the length of the gap between decking boards—$8\frac{1}{2}$ inches for 18-inch shakes; $11\frac{1}{2}$ inches for 24-inch shakes—and use it to align the bottom of each shake with that of the shake in the course below.

◆ Lay an 18-inch strip of roofing felt with its lower edge halfway between the top of the starter course and the bottom of the next course.

◆ Fasten the second course of shakes with two 2-inch box nails *(left)*.

◆ Lay another strip of felt, then another course of shakes. Continue in this way to the ridge.

◆ With 3-inch box nails, cover the ridge with special two-piece ridge shakes: Start by doubling the ridge shakes at one end, then overlap the shakes as you move along the ridge to the other end so the corner joints alternate from one side of the ridge to the other *(inset)*.

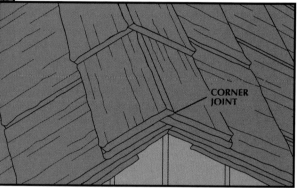

CORNER JOINT

Making Shakes

You may want to cut your own shakes from cedar or redwood logs. To do so, saw a log into 16-inch sections and mark lines at $\frac{1}{4}$-inch intervals across the end of the section. Place the log on wood blocks, hold a frow—a special cutter available from specialty-tool suppliers—with its sharp edge against the top of the log, and strike the blade sharply with a wooden mallet *(right)*, severing the shake from the log. Do not try to cut through a knot; instead, remove the frow and move to the next mark on the log.

TRICKS OF THE TRADE

Log cabins are built with construction techniques all their own. Instead of stud or A-frame walls, logs are stacked one on top of another and notched to interlock at the corners.

Choosing the Timber: Log-cabin kits that include plans and precut logs are available, but you can save considerable expense if you obtain and prepare the logs yourself. Choose softwoods—cedar, pine, fir, or larch—that measure 8 to 12 inches in diameter and taper very little from butt to tip. To calculate the number of logs you will need, divide the combined heights in inches of all the walls in your plan—including gables at the end walls—by the average diameter in inches of the logs. Add a few extra logs to your total to allow for errors.

Preparing the Logs: You can fell trees on your own property *(pages 10-12)*; in some areas, you can log land of the National Forests or of a local lumber company after paying a "stumpage fee." You may be able to buy ready-to-use logs from a local utility or logging company.

Allow green logs to dry for at least six months. To prevent excessive cracking of the wood during the drying process, use a spud *(below)* to peel a 2-inch strip along each log from two opposite sides; any cracking that occurs will be confined to these strips, and will be concealed as you build. Peel the bark from the rest of the log to help protect against insect damage. Stack the logs in two layers, spacing them about 3 inches apart to allow for air circulation between them. Cover them with pine boughs and turn them every month or so to prevent uneven drying.

Building a Foundation: A log cabin requires a block-wall foundation *(pages 24-33)* with modifications: To compensate for the fact that the first course of logs on the front and back walls are higher than that of the side walls by one log diameter, the foundation at the front and back is built up by a course of cored half blocks. In addition, the anchor bolts embedded in the foundation must be long enough to penetrate the first course of logs and the sill plate.

   TOOLS

Log dogs	Electric drill
Chain saw	Spade bit (1½")
Lumber-cutting	Extension bit (¾")
jig	Socket wrench
2 x 4 guide	Scribers
Hammer	Gouge chisel
	Mallet
	Caulking gun

 **MATERIALS**

Logs	Joist hangers
2 x 8s	and nails
Exterior-grade ply-	Anchor bolt
wood (¾")	washers and
Common nails	nuts
(3½")	Sill seal
Ring-shank nails	Polyethylene
(2½")	sheeting
	(6-mil)
	Bricks

SAFETY TIPS

Wear a hard hat, hearing protection, goggles or a face shield, work gloves, and steel-toed boots when operating a chain saw. Protect your eyes with goggles when chiseling notches in logs.

TIME-HONORED CABIN-BUILDING TOOLS

The chain saw has replaced many of the tools once used in log-cabin construction, but a few traditional implements, available from specialized tool or antique dealers, remain essential. The double-handled drawknife is pulled along logs to smooth their surfaces. The cant hook, a pole with a spiked hook at one end, makes it easy to drag heavy logs short distances. The peeling spud, with its shovel-like blade, strips bark off logs. Log dogs are 3-foot iron bars with turned points at each end. The points are driven into a log and a nearby support to secure the log while you work on it. You'll need at least four dogs for building a log cabin. Instead of buying them, you may want to make your own *(page 71)*.

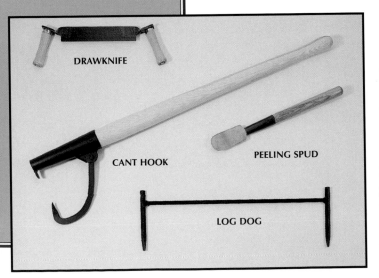

DRAWKNIFE

CANT HOOK

PEELING SPUD

LOG DOG

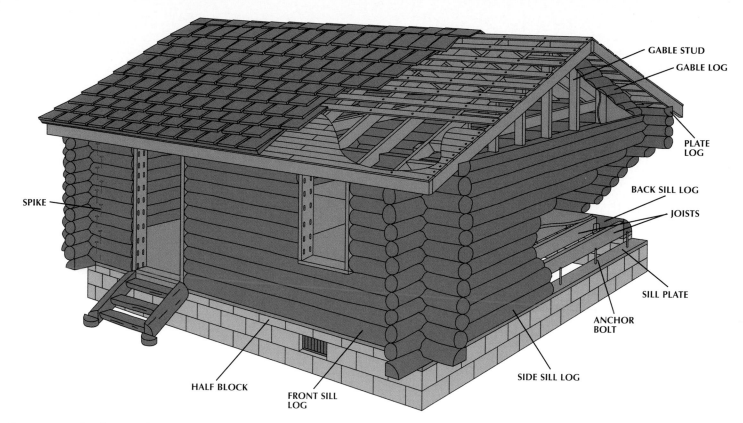

SPIKE

GABLE STUD

GABLE LOG

PLATE LOG

BACK SILL LOG

JOISTS

SILL PLATE

ANCHOR BOLT

SIDE SILL LOG

HALF BLOCK

FRONT SILL LOG

Anatomy of a log cabin.

The masonry-block foundation for this cabin is identical to the one on pages 24 to 31, except that the front and back walls are topped with an extra course of half blocks and the anchor bolts are longer, as explained opposite. Pressure-treated 2-by-8s form the sill plates, and split and squared-off sill logs are attached with anchor bolts to the foundation. The side sill logs are installed first, then the front and back sill logs are notched to fit over them; 2-by-8 floor joists supported by joist hangers run between the back and front sill logs. Logs notched at the corners form the walls, and are held in place by spikes driven 2 feet from every corner and on both sides of door and window openings. On top of the front and back walls, plate logs with squared top and outside faces simplify the notching of rafter lumber at the roof. Gable logs are fastened to gable studs. The roof is put on last *(pages 77-81 and 64-67).*

LAYING DOWN THE SIDE SILL LOGS

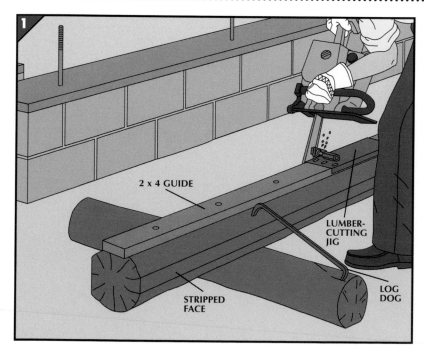

2 x 4 GUIDE

LUMBER-CUTTING JIG

STRIPPED FACE

LOG DOG

1. Flattening the side sill logs.

◆ Set a log on two scrap timbers with one of its stripped faces away from you and secure it with a log dog at each end.

◆ Attach a 2-by-4 guide as long as the log along its top with $3\frac{1}{2}$-inch common nails, positioning the guide so a chain saw will leave a 3- to 4-inch-wide flat strip when it runs along the guide and log.

◆ Bolt a commercial lumber-cutting jig *(page 70)* to a chain saw and clamp the device to the guide at one end of the log.

◆ Turn on the saw and run it with the jig along the log and guide *(left),* stopping at the opposite end.

◆ Remove the guide, turn the log over 90 degrees, and repeat the process to flatten an adjacent side, and two adjacent sides of the other side sill log.

SQUARING LOGS WITH A LUMBER-CUTTING JIG

Flattening or squaring logs with just a chain saw can be arduous work, and often results in uneven surfaces. Paired with a lumber-cutting jig, however, a saw can transform a felled tree into boards of any size in just minutes. Lightweight and easy to use, the jig has a U-shaped clamp with two bolts that attach to the chain saw guide bar. The jig is sized to hug the edges of a guide board fastened to the log and run along them as the saw cuts off one side of the log. The placement of the guide board determines the width of the cut.

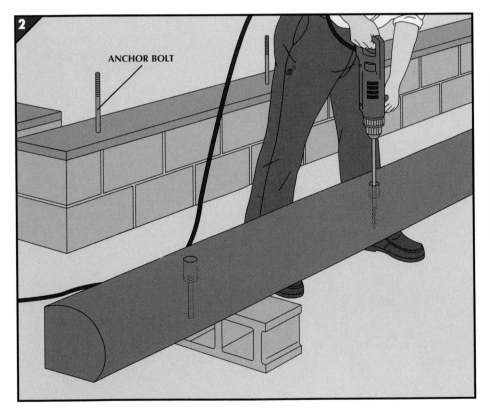

ANCHOR BOLT

2. Drilling the side sill logs.
◆ Transfer the anchor-bolt locations from the sill to the side sill logs as for the sill plate *(page 30, Step 1)*.
◆ Drill a 2-inch-deep hole into the logs at each bolt location with a $\frac{1}{2}$-inch electric drill fitted with a $1\frac{1}{2}$-inch spade bit.
◆ Extend each hole through the logs with a $\frac{3}{4}$-inch electrician's extension bit *(left)*.

SIDE SILL LOG

SILL PLATE

3. Anchoring the side sill logs.

◆ Position the side sill logs on their sill plates, slipping the holes over the anchor bolts.
◆ Install the anchor bolts' washers and nuts and tighten the nuts with a socket wrench *(left)*.
◆ Seal gaps between the sill logs and sill plates with sill seal, caulk, or water-impermeable foam gasket.
◆ Starting 8 inches from the end of each sill plate, mark a joist position across the sill logs every 16 inches.
◆ With metal joist hangers, fasten joists to the sill logs at the marks.

TRICKS OF THE TRADE

Homemade Log Dogs

Instead of buying metal log dogs, you can make your own from 2-by-4s cut 18 inches long. Drill a $\frac{1}{2}$-inch pilot hole through a 2-by-4 2 inches from each end and nail a 6-inch spike through the hole. When securing a dog to a log, hammer the heads of the spikes rather than the 2-by-4s; otherwise, the spikes may be pushed up through the top of the holes.

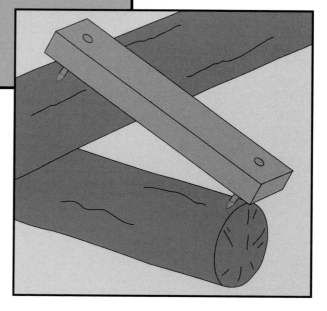

FITTING THE FRONT AND BACK SILL LOGS

1. Marking the notches.

◆ Set the front sill log on the sill plate across the side sill logs and secure it with log dogs.

◆ Adjust the points on a pair of scribers to one-half the log diameter. This measurement will leave the smallest practical gap between logs as you raise the walls; for a larger gap, decrease the distance between the scriber points, but avoid a gap larger than 2 inches.

◆ Place one point on the outside of the front sill log and the other against the top of the side sill log. Keeping the points in a vertical line (as indicated by the dashed line in the illustration) and in contact with both logs, follow the contours of the front sill log, scratching its profile on the side sill log *(right)*.

◆ Repeat on the opposite side of the front sill log and on both sides at the other end.

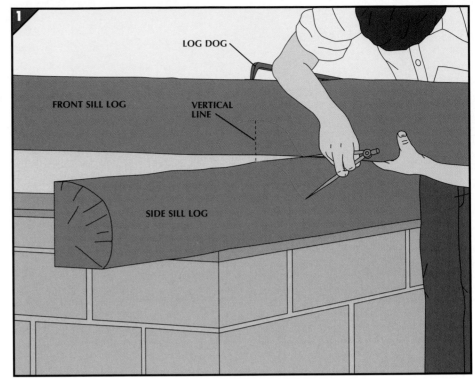

2. Cutting the notches.

◆ Remove the log dogs, turn the front sill log over, and resecure it.

◆ With a chain saw, make a series of vertical cuts at 1-inch intervals into the log within each notch outline, stopping just short of the scribed lines *(above, left)*.

◆ Cut out the waste wood to the lines with a 2-inch beveled gouge chisel and a mallet *(above, right)*.

◆ Turn the log over and mark any high spots where the notches do not rest flush on the side sill log. Rotate and secure the log again, trim any high spots with the gouge or a drawknife *(page 68)*, then reposition the log.

◆ Fit the back sill log on the opposite sill plate in the same way.

◆ Attach 2-by-8 joists to the sill logs with joist hangers, and install a vapor barrier and subfloor *(page 33, Steps 4-5)*.

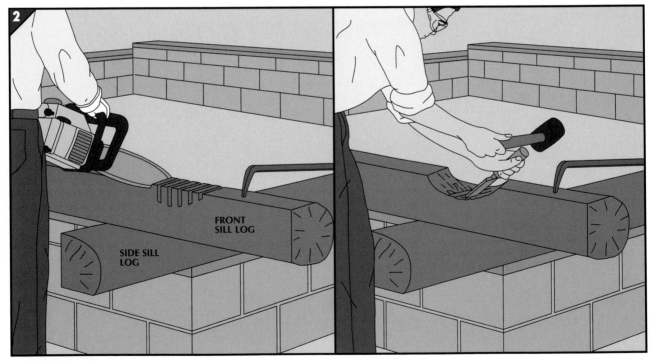

Unlike the precise measuring and planning involved in building walls with milled lumber, raising a log wall is a process of approximating and compensating. Choosing like-sized logs for corresponding positions in opposite walls helps keep the walls level. Use matched pairs of thick logs at the bottom of opposite walls, pair off thinner logs near the top. To compensate for the logs' natural taper, alternate the thick ends—called butts—within each wall.

Leveling the Courses: Check the level of the walls every second course—every odd-numbered course if the cabin will have an odd number—by measuring the front and back walls from the subfloor to the top of each wall at the corners of the cabin. If the measurements vary by more than 1 inch, place a log with thin or thick ends as needed, or adjust the depth of the next corner notch. A shallow notch will lift the end of a wall that is beginning to dip; a deeper notch will lower it. Deepen notches with care, however; a log notched too deeply rests along its length on the log below, and a structurally unsound gap appears at the top of the notch.

Doors and Windows: To install doors and windows made from scratch or bought prehung, you will need to cut and frame openings in the logs *(pages 75-76)* that match the size of the doors and windows, including jambs. The special construction of the frames allows the walls to settle gradually without racking the doors and windows.

TOOLS

Electric drill
Spade bit ($1\frac{1}{2}$")
Extension bit ($\frac{1}{2}$")
Hammer
Machine bolt
Lumber-cutting jig

2 x 4 guide
Chain saw
Drawknife
Carpenter's level
Wood chisel
Mallet
Caulking gun

MATERIALS

2 x 4s, 2 x 8s
Spikes ($\frac{3}{8}$" x 8")
Washers ($\frac{1}{2}$")
Rope
Common nails ($2\frac{1}{2}$")

Galvanized common
 nails ($3\frac{1}{2}$")
Doors, windows,
 and shims
Insulation
Caulk

SAFETY TIPS

Goggles protect your eyes when you are hammering. Wear a hard hat, hearing protection, goggles or a face shield, work gloves, and steel-toed boots when operating a chain saw.

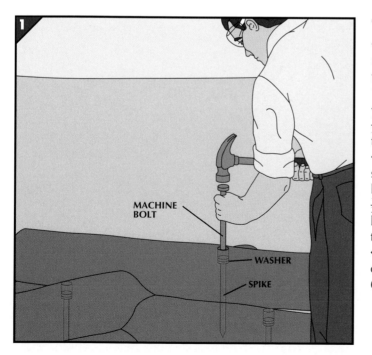

MACHINE BOLT

WASHER

SPIKE

1. Spiking the logs.

◆ After laying the first course of logs atop the sill logs, notching them as you did the sill logs *(page 72)*, mark holes for spikes on the logs about 2 feet from each corner and 1 foot from each side of a planned window or door opening.
◆ At each mark, drill a $1\frac{1}{2}$-inch-diameter hole at least $\frac{1}{2}$ inch deep into the log, then use a $\frac{1}{2}$-inch extension bit to extend each hole halfway through the log.
◆ For each hole, use petroleum jelly to grease a $\frac{3}{8}$-inch spike long enough to reach from the bottom of the wider hole to the middle of the log in the course below. Slip a $\frac{1}{2}$-inch washer on the spike, then drive the spike into the hole with a hammer and a long machine bolt *(left)*. Mark the spike locations on the sides of the logs.
◆ Drive spikes into each successive log in the same way, offsetting them from those in the course below by 4 to 6 inches.

MARKS FOR DOOR OR WINDOW OPENING

2. Rolling logs up a wall.

◆ When the walls get too high to lift the logs into place by hand, prop a pole against each end of the wall at a 45-degree angle.

◆ Spike the poles to the ends of the top-course logs of the adjoining walls.

◆ Tie two ropes around the top log of the wall and loop the ropes under the next log.

◆ With a helper, pull the free ends of the ropes to roll the log up the poles *(left)*.

◆ When the highest log that will have to be cut for a door or window opening is in position, saw a V-shaped notch into its top just inside each side of the planned opening *(inset)*. Make the notches deep enough to accommodate the chain saw's blade when the next course is laid.

3. Squaring the plate logs.

◆ For the plate logs—those at the top of the front and back walls—choose two logs with little or no taper.

◆ Set one plate log on a scrap timber and secure it with a log dog.

◆ With a chain saw, guide board, and lumber-cutting jig *(page 69, Step 1)*, square one side of the log *(right)*, then turn the log 90 degrees and square an adjoining face so the two surfaces form a right angle. Trim and smooth the cuts with a drawknife, as necessary.

◆ Cut the second plate log in the same way.

LUMBER-CUTTING JIG

GUIDE BOARD

FRAMING DOORS AND WINDOWS

1. Nailing up guide strips.

◆ For each door or window opening, cut two 2-by-4 guide strips 18 inches longer than the height of the door or window unit.

◆ With a $2\frac{1}{2}$-inch common nail, tack the top of a strip to an interior wall on each side of the planned opening at least 6 inches above the top of the opening. Position the strips so a chain saw will cut through the center of the wall notches with a lumber-cutting jig running along the strips.

◆ With a carpenter's level, plumb each strip *(right)*, then drive two more nails.

◆ Fasten strips to the exterior wall that align with the interior strips.

◆ Mark level lines across the interior walls for the top and bottom of each opening: For a door unit, measure up from the subfloor a distance of 5 inches greater than the height of the unit; mark the top and bottom of window opening with lines as far apart as the height of the window unit plus 6 inches. Avoid locating the bottom of a window between two logs.

◆ Drive a tapered shim on each side of the openings between the logs you'll be sawing to prevent the cut ends from sagging.

GUIDE STRIPS

SHIM

MARK FOR TOP OF WINDOW OPENING

2. Cutting out the opening.

◆ Attach a lumber-cutting jig to a chain saw and to the interior guide on the left side of the opening.

◆ Starting at the notch at the top of the opening, run the chain saw along the guide and cut through the first log.

◆ Attach the jig to the guide on the opposite side of the opening and cut through the same log. Remove the waste section and square the ends of the logs where the notches were located.

◆ Complete the opening, cutting the logs one at a time *(left)*. Stop when you have removed the last full log, then remove the guide strips.

CHAIN-SAW CUT

3. Squaring the opening.
◆ At the top and bottom of the opening, saw a series of vertical cuts at 1-inch intervals to the marked lines on the wall.
◆ Cut away the waste wood between the cuts with a wood chisel and mallet *(left)*.
◆ Smooth the cut surfaces with a drawknife, making them flat for a window or prehung door; slanting slightly outward for a homemade door.

SLOT

TRICKS OF THE TRADE

Flexible Frames

Instead of cutting slots in door and window frames to allow log walls to settle, you can cut dadoes 1 inch deep and wide with a router or circular saw across the ends of the logs on each side of window or door openings. Then, cut matching dadoes along the sides of the frame and join the frame pieces to the logs with splines that fit

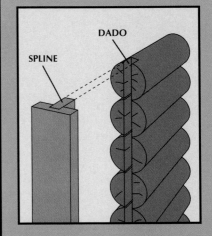

SPLINE

DADO

the dadoes snugly. Because the frames are not fixed to the logs, they will remain square if the logs settle or shrink.

WINDOW FRAME

4. Framing the openings.
◆ Build a rough 2-by-8 frame as wide as the opening and high enough to leave 3 inches of air space above a door frame and 2 inches above a window frame. Join the frame together with $3\frac{1}{2}$-inch galvanized common nails *(above)*.
◆ Position the frame in the wall opening with its inner edges flush with the interior wall. Plumb the frame and tack it to the logs.
◆ At each log adjoining the opening, drill a series of linked holes

through the side jamb with a $\frac{7}{16}$-inch bit to form two vertical slots about 2 inches wide. The slots allow the logs to settle without pulling the frames down with them.
◆ Drive an 8-inch spike through the top of each slot *(inset)*, then remove the shims you drove in Step 1.
◆ Fill in the space above the opening with a compressible insulating material such as fiberglass. Outside, cover the space with trim attached to the header, but not the jamb. Caulk around the trim.

When the log walls are completed, you can turn to the job of roofing and closing in the cabin. Most of the roof framing is done with lumber rather than logs; the boards are all cut on the ground and then lifted into place. To make the above-ground work easier and safer, rent two scaffolds—one for each end of the cabin.

Framing the Roof: Begin the job by choosing a roof slope appropriate for the climate and the roofing material *(pages 64 and 96)*. You can purchase boards for the framing or mill them from logs with a chain saw and a lumber-cutting jig *(page 70)*. The width of rafter lumber depends on the distance the rafters will span, as well as how far apart they are spaced. Find the correct size for your cabin using the chart on page 56, selecting boards that are long enough to create the overhang you want at the eaves.

Sealing the Gaps: After the roof is finished, fill all the gaps between the logs of the walls with foam backer rod sealed with adhesive chinking. The rod is available at building-supply stores; buy adhesive chinking through mail-order catalogs of log-cabin supplies. You can close in the cabin with a ready-made door, or you can build a rustic door that complements the log walls *(page 82)*.

TOOLS

Scaffolds	Sawhorses	Chain saw
Circular saw	Crosscut saw	Lumber-cutting jig
Hammer	Paintbrush	2 x 4 guide
Chalk line	Caulking gun	Drawknife
	Screwdriver	
	Staple gun	

MATERIALS

	Logs	Roof sheathing
1 x 2s, 1 x 4s,	Common nails	Roofing materials
1 x 6s, 1 x 8s	(2", 3")	Resin log stain
2 x 4s, 2 x 6s,	Galvanized	Foam backer rod
2 x 8s	common	Adhesive chinking
Rafter lumber	nails (3")	Wood glue
Tongue-and-groove	Galvanized box	Building paper
boards ($\frac{3}{4}$" x 8")	nails ($2\frac{1}{2}$")	Construction
Exterior-grade	Finishing nails (1")	adhesive
plywood ($\frac{3}{4}$")	Wood screws	Strap hinges
	(2", 3" No. 8)	

SAFETY TIPS

Goggles protect your eyes when you are hammering or using power tools.

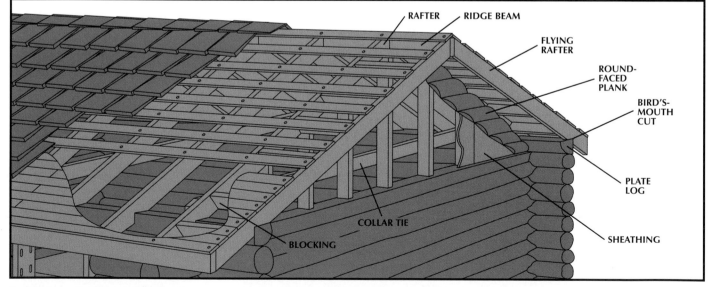

Anatomy of a log-cabin roof.

The roof of this log cabin is built of rafters fastened to a 2-by-8 ridge beam and to the plate logs on top of the walls. The rafters are mitered to fit against the ridge beam, and a notch called a bird's-mouth cut lets them sit securely on the plate logs. Blocking at the end rafters helps fortify the "flying" rafters of the roof's overhang. To counteract the outward push of the roof on the log walls, collar ties of 2-by-6s are installed at every third rafter. Sheathing and round-faced planks, rather than whole logs, are used to build the gable walls to prevent them from settling and causing the roof to sag.

1. Building ridge-beam supports.

◆ At each gable wall, set up a scaffold inside the cabin. Metal scaffolding, available at tool rental centers, can be adjusted for work at various heights.
◆ Build a support for each end of the ridge beam: Cut a 1-by-6 about 2 feet longer than the planned height of the roof peak and nail it to a pair of 1-by-2s cut 14 inches long, extending $7\frac{1}{2}$ inches above

the top of the 1-by-6 and spaced $1\frac{1}{2}$ inches apart.
◆ Center the support board between the plate logs with the tops of the cleats at the planned height of the roof peak and fasten it to the inside of each gable wall with 3-inch common nails (above).
◆ Nail a 1-by-4 diagonally from the gable wall to each of the support boards to brace them.

2. Raising the ridge beam.

◆ Cut a 2-by-8 ridge beam the length of the cabin plus the width of the desired gable overhang of 1 to 3 feet.
◆ Mark the rafter positions on both sides of the ridge beam according to rafter spacing appropriate for your cabin (page 56), aligning the outer marks with the gable walls.
◆ With a helper, raise the ridge beam to the scaffolding and cradle it in its supports with the proper overhang at each end (left).

1. Marking the first rafter.

◆ Snap a chalk line down the middle of a length of rafter lumber of the appropriate size *(page 56)*.
◆ With a helper, position the board against the ridge beam and plate log at one gable wall so the board overhangs the eave wall by the correct amount and the chalk line is level with the outside corner of the log. Position the upper end so the top edge is flush with the top of the ridge beam.
◆ Mark the inside of the ridge beam on the board *(above)*.
◆ Tack the board to the ridge beam, and have your helper tack it to the plate log, then outline the plate log on the rafter.

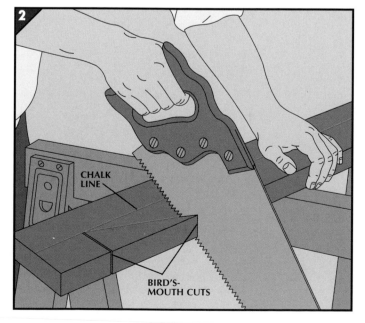

2. Cutting the rafters.

◆ Set the marked board on sawhorses and trim it at the ridge-beam mark with a circular saw or crosscut saw.
◆ Make the bird's-mouth notch along the outline of the plate log with two cuts: Saw along the vertical line to the chalk line, then make the diagonal cut *(left)*, stopping at the end of the first cut.
◆ Use the board as a template to mark and cut the remaining rafters, making one for each mark on the ridge beam, including the flying rafters that frame the overhang at each end of the cabin.

FLYING RAFTER

3. Attaching the rafters.
◆ With two helpers—one holding a rafter on its outline on the ridge beam, the other keeping it aligned and in position on the plate log—fasten a flying rafter to the beam with two 3-inch common nails *(above)*. In a high-wind area, use hurricane ties *(page 92)*.
◆ Have a helper toenail the rafter to the plate log.
◆ Nail a 1-by-4 from the rafter to the gable wall as a temporary brace.
◆ Repeat the procedure to toenail a flying rafter to the other side of the ridge beam, then install the flying rafters at the opposite end of the cabin in the same way.
◆ Nail the remaining rafters in place, temporarily bracing each one with a 1-by-4 nailed to the last one installed.

4. Adding the collar ties.
◆ Cut a 2-by-6 collar tie to span between the ends of the rafters.
◆ With a helper, position the collar tie across the plate logs, flat against one set of end rafters, and mark the top edge of each rafter on the tie *(right)*.
◆ Cut the collar tie along the marks.
◆ Use the board as a template to mark and cut a collar tie for every third set of rafters.
◆ With 3-inch common nails, fasten a collar tie to each set of end rafters and to every third set in between.
◆ Remove the rafter bracing and the ridge-beam supports.

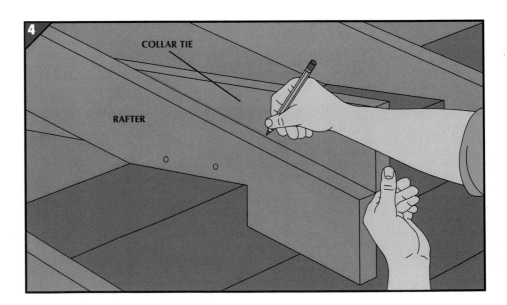

COLLAR TIE

RAFTER

FRAMING THE GABLE ENDS

1. Framing gable ends.

◆ At equal intervals—up to a maximum of 24 inches—along the end rafters, measure from the top edge of the rafter straight down to the top of the gable wall.

◆ Cut a 2-by-4 gable stud for each measurement, mitering the top end to match the roof slope. Cut a notch halfway through the stud thickness at the top end to fit behind the rafter.

◆ With 3-inch common nails, toenail the stud to the top of the wall. Fasten the stud to the rafter with two 2-inch nails through the notch *(right)*.

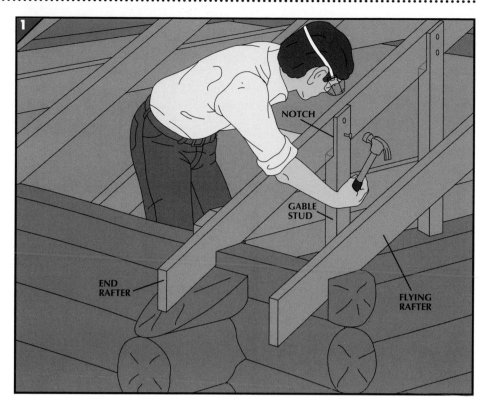

2. Framing the gable overhang.

◆ Cut enough lengths of blocking from rafter lumber to fit between the end rafters and flying rafters at 16-inch intervals.

◆ With a helper holding the blocking in position, fasten a length to the rafters every 16 inches with 3-inch nails *(left)*.

◆ Sheathe the gable ends with two layers of material. First, fasten $\frac{7}{16}$-inch exterior-grade plywood to the gable studs with $2\frac{1}{2}$-inch galvanized box nails *(page 40, Step 5)*. Then cover the plywood with round-faced 2-inch-thick planks *(page 83, Step 2)*. Miter the ends of the planks to match the roof slope, then fasten them edge to edge to the plywood with 3-inch galvanized nails.

◆ For the roof, lay down sheathing as for an A-frame *(page 47, Step 3)*. Then fasten any of the roofing materials described on pages 64 to 67.

SEALING THE WALLS

Filling the gaps between logs.

◆ Clean and dry all log surfaces on both sides of the gaps between logs and between log ends and door or window frames.

◆ Brush resin log stain on the cleaned surfaces to prime them for the adhesive chinking that will fill the gaps.

◆ Buy foam backer rod of a size that will fit snugly in the gaps, then push one length in. If necessary, drive a 1-inch finishing nail through the rod and into a log every 4 feet to secure it.

◆ Cover the rod by applying a bead of adhesive chinking along the logs with a caulking gun *(right)*.

◆ Fill the remaining gaps in the same way.

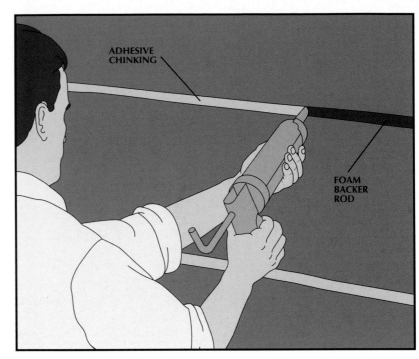

BUILDING AND HANGING DOORS

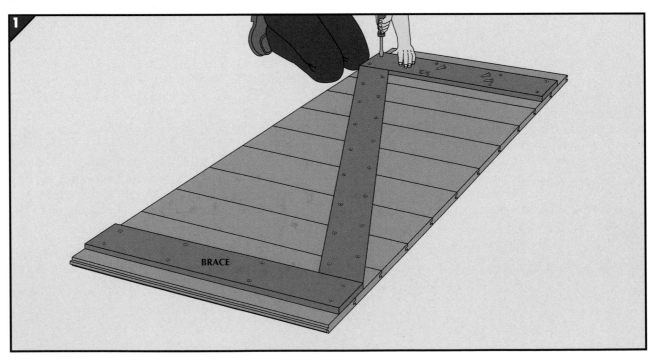

BRACE

1. Making the core.

◆ Trim lengths of $\frac{3}{4}$-by-8-inch tongue-and-groove stock $\frac{1}{4}$ inch shorter than the width of the door frame, cutting enough lengths to form a door at least $1\frac{1}{2}$ inches higher than its frame.

◆ Spread wood glue on the tongues and grooves and fit the pieces together.

◆ Cut two 1-by-8s to the width of the door and center them along the joints at the top and bottom of the assembly. Cut a third 1-by-8, mitering its ends to fit diagonally between the first two boards. With 2-inch No. 8 wood screws, fasten the three boards in a Z pattern to brace the door *(above)*.

◆ Cut the door $\frac{1}{4}$ inch shorter than its frame, trimming equal amounts from the top and bottom.

◆ Staple building paper to the flat face of the door.

2. Adding a log facade.

◆ With a chain saw and a lumber-cutting jig *(page 69, Step 1)*, cut round-faced 2-inch-thick planks from logs $\frac{3}{4}$ inch shorter than the height of the door. Cut enough lengths to cover the face of the door.

◆ Set the planks edge to edge on the door *(left)*, then measure how much the outside pieces extend beyond the edge.

3. Trimming the slabs.

◆ Holding a plank on edge between your legs, use a drawknife to trim the edge *(right)*. Remove the same amount of wood from each edge of all the planks so the outside pieces will be flush with the door edges.

◆ Apply construction adhesive to the back of each plank, then place them on the face of the door so the bottom ends are flush with the bottom of the door. Fasten the planks with 3-inch No. 8 wood screws driven into the middle of each plank and spaced 6 inches apart—or use cut nails *(photograph)* to give the cabin a rustic appearance.

◆ Fasten heavy-duty strap hinges to the back of the door and to the inside edge of the door frame *(left inset)*. Three hinges are recommended to hang heavy doors.

◆ After hanging the door, position and nail 1-by-2 doorstops on the inside of the door frame *(right inset)*.

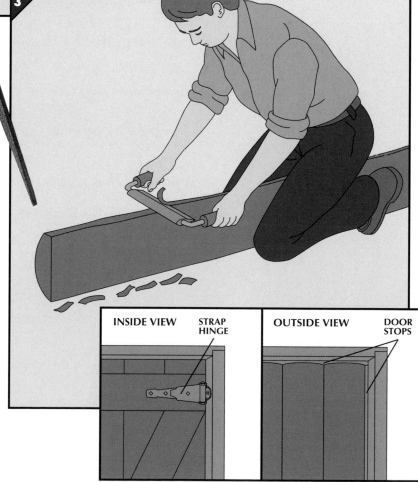

| INSIDE VIEW | STRAP HINGE | OUTSIDE VIEW | DOOR STOPS |

Making the Best of Nature's Worst

The features that make some vacation retreats desirable—such as a nearby lake, river, or ocean; or a region covered by deep snow in winter—can also make a location a poor building site. But even in these areas, you can still choose the safest spot to place your cabin, and you can add elements that strengthen or protect the structure as you build.

Earthquakes occur in many parts of North America with enough force to shake a building to pieces. If you plan to build a vacation home in any of these areas *(map, below)*, you will need to reinforce the structure.

A Solid Base: Begin with a masonry-block foundation *(pages 24-33)*, but stiffen it with a skeleton of $\frac{5}{8}$-inch steel reinforcing bars and fill the block cores with concrete grout *(pages 87-89)*. Vertical rebars cast into the footing provide a strong anchor; depending on the height of the wall and on local code, you may also need special masonry units called bond-beam blocks that permit rebar to run horizontally inside the walls and round the corners without interruption. Check codes to determine which courses need bond-beam blocks and horizontal rebar.

Make grade pegs 16 inches long. To fashion the vertical supports, bend rebar *(page 26)* at a right angle 6 inches from one end and cut it long enough to extend 25 inches above the top of the footing. Bend horizontal bars sharply to turn corners. For skirting vents *(page 88, Step 2)*, order rebar prebent.

For mortar strong enough to maintain a good bond during tremors, mix $2\frac{1}{2}$ gallons of Portland cement, $1\frac{1}{4}$ gallons of hydrated lime, and $8\frac{3}{4}$ gallons of sand for each cubic foot of mortar mix. Buy premixed grout, or blend 1 gallon of cement, $2\frac{1}{2}$ gallons of sand, $1\frac{1}{2}$ gallons of coarse aggregate, and $\frac{1}{2}$ gallon of water.

Additional Protection: A strong foundation alone does not provide enough support for a cabin with stud walls. You can brace the walls with plywood sheathing *(page 90)*.

If the cabin's heating unit or cookstove is fueled by gas, have a qualified technician install an earthquake valve *(page 90)* to reduce the danger of fire from a ruptured line.

TOOLS

Maul	Rebar cutter	Mason's line
Hammer	Square-edged shovel	Tin snips
Shovel	Wooden float	Brickset
Plumb bob	Chalk line	Ball-peen hammer
Water level	Mason's trowel	Circular saw
	Mason's level	

MATERIALS

1 x 2s, 1 x 6s
2 x 4s
Plywood ($\frac{3}{8}$")
Exterior plywood siding ($\frac{7}{16}$")
Ring-shank nails ($2\frac{1}{2}$")
Galvanized box nails (2")
Powdered chalk
Concrete mix
Mortar mix

Rebar ($\frac{5}{8}$"), supports, and safety caps
Mechanic's wire (16-gauge)
Polyethylene sheeting
Concrete blocks
Bond-beam blocks
Metal mesh
Vents
Grout
Anchor bolts ($\frac{1}{2}$" x 8"), washers, and nuts

SAFETY TIPS

Wear goggles and a dust mask when mixing mortar. Put on heavy gloves and work boots when working with concrete blocks, and goggles to cut blocks or pour grout.

Seismic areas.

In this map of North America, dark red sections represent areas where the risk of severe earthquakes is greatest. If you are building in these zones, the special building techniques on the following pages are advisable. In light red areas, major earthquakes are less likely but still possible; consult local building codes to find out whether reinforcement is necessary. Orange, yellow, green, or beige areas represent a decreasing likelihood of seismic activity, and in pink areas, earthquakes are rare and codes usually require no additional reinforcement for new construction.

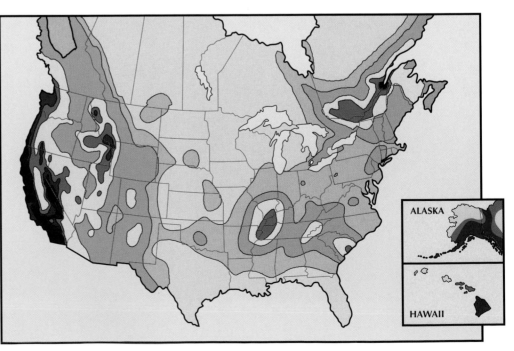

BOLSTERING A FOUNDATION WALL

1. Supporting vertical rebar.

◆ Dig the footing trench and lay $\frac{5}{8}$-inch horizontal reinforcement *(pages 24-26)*.

◆ Tie a string between the batterboards to mark the center of the planned wall.

◆ Cut two short pieces of rebar for cross ties and lash the ties across the horizontal rebar 16 inches apart—or spaced according to building codes. Omit ties where you will lay solid blocks under girder pockets.

◆ With 16-gauge mechanic's wire, lash prebent vertical rebars to the cross ties as tightly as possible *(right)*.

◆ When all the bars are wired in place, pour the footing *(page 26, Step 5)*, keeping the vertical rebar straight.

◆ Place a safety cap over each vertical rebar to prevent injury while you are building the wall.

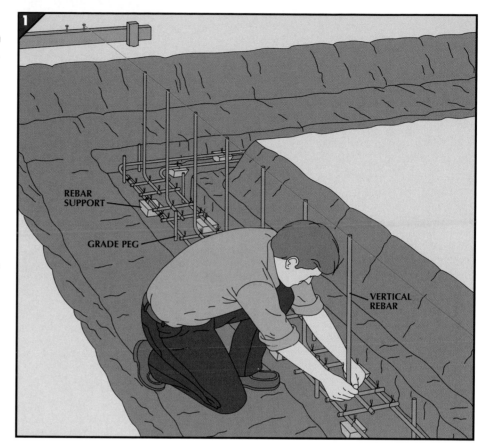

REBAR SUPPORT

GRADE PEG

VERTICAL REBAR

A QUICK MIX FOR MORTAR

You can simplify the job of preparing mortar with a rented portable electric mortar mixer *(right)*. This model, with large tires for negotiating rough terrain, is light and easy to move. Shovel the dry ingredients into the drum, then add water gradually until the mix has the desired consistency. Position a container under the chute to catch the mortar when you discharge it from the mixer.

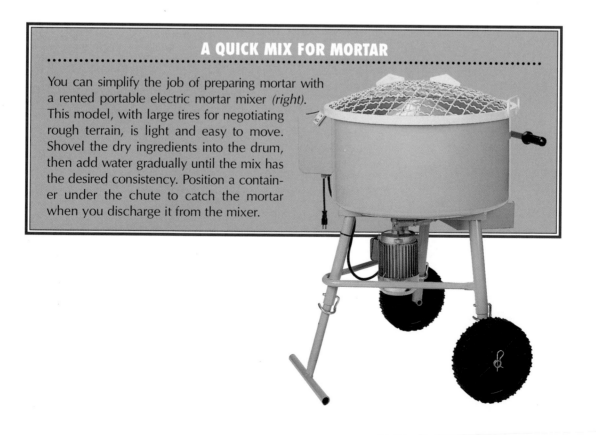

SAFETY CAP

2. Building the first courses.

◆ Spread a 10-inch-wide and 1½-inch-thick mortar bed on the footing, then start building the foundation at each corner of the footing *(page 27, Step 1)*, placing the blocks over the vertical rebar.

◆ Level the blocks *(page 27, Step 2)*.

◆ Lay the subsequent courses in the same way *(left)*, omitting the mesh at every third course as in a standard block-wall foundation, until a bond-beam course is called for. Add vents as necessary *(page 28, Step 3)*, placing rebar that has been prebent and cut to length to skirt the vents.

3. Making bond-beam corner blocks.

Adapt a standard corner block to allow horizontal rebar to turn each corner in a bond-beam course: With a brickset and ball-peen hammer, chisel the middle web and the webs that will abut blocks at the corner *(right)* to the level of the webs in a bond-beam block.

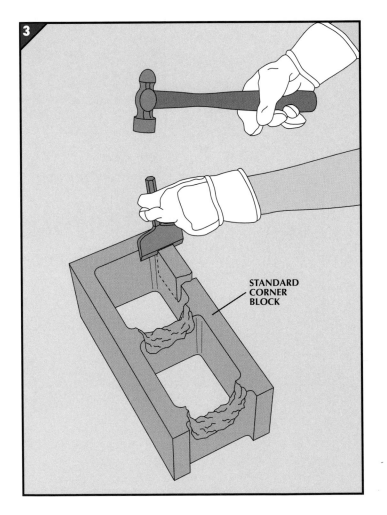

STANDARD CORNER BLOCK

4. Making a bond beam.

◆ With tin snips, cut pieces of metal mesh to fit over one core of each standard block.

◆ Embed the mesh in mortar over every block core without vertical rebar, then lay a course of bond-beam blocks *(photograph)* as for standard blocks, placing the modified corner blocks at each corner and solid blocks for girder pockets as for a standard wall.

◆ Remove the safety caps from the ends of the vertical rebars.

◆ On the webs of the bond-beam blocks around the entire course, set two rebars parallel to each other and 2 inches apart. Bend the rebars to turn the corners and overlap 12 inches at each end. Cut the rebars at the solid blocks below the girder pockets.

◆ With 16-gauge mechanic's wire, fasten the overlapped ends together *(above)*.

◆ If the bond-beam course is the top course in the wall, grout it *(Step 5)*. If it is an intermediate course, wire a second length of vertical rebar to

the end of each existing piece of vertical rebar, overlapping the bars 30 inches and with the second piece extending 16 inches. Cover each one with a safety cap, and continue adding courses of standard block as in Step 2.

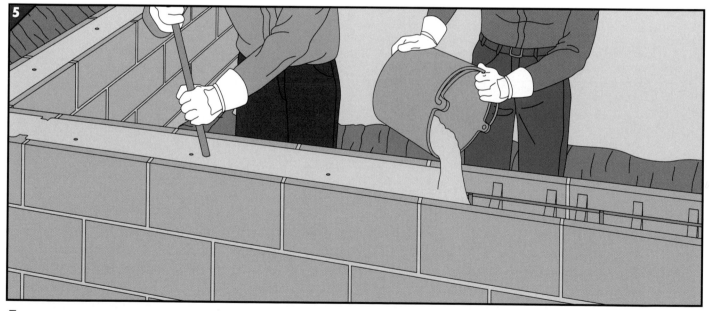

5. Grouting the wall.

◆ Before mixing and pouring grout, prepare to embed anchor bolts for the sill plate in the grout *(page 28, Step 5)*. If you plan to brace the cabin against wind with anchor-downs, make the bolts at door and window

openings long enough to pass through the soleplates of the stud walls *(page 91, Step 1)*.

◆ Pour grout into all the cores containing vertical rebar and into the bond-beam blocks. Have a helper follow to compact the grout with a

stick to remove air pockets *(above)*. (The mesh placed over the cores without rebar in Step 4 will keep the grout from filling those cores.)

◆ With a mason's trowel, strike off the grout flush with the tops of the bond-beam blocks.

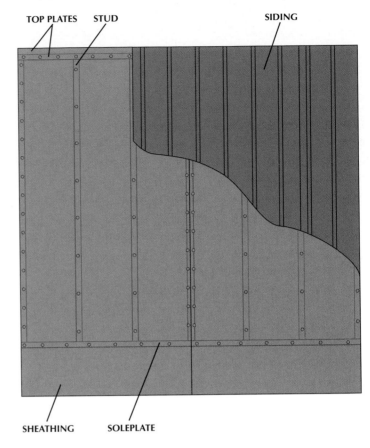

Adding sheathing.

Assemble and put up walls in the same way you would for prefabricated walls *(pages 38-41, Steps 1-7)*, but instead of nailing on only siding, first fasten $\frac{3}{8}$-inch plywood sheathing. Space the panels $\frac{1}{8}$ inch apart and nail them to the studs, top plate, and soleplate every 6 inches around the perimeter, and every 12 inches in between with 2-inch box nails. If your cabin is in an area subject to earthquakes or hurricanes, check local codes; the sheathing may need to be thicker and the nails spaced closer together—from 2 to 4 inches apart. Fasten $\frac{7}{16}$-inch exterior siding to the sheathing with $2\frac{1}{2}$-inch galvanized nails driven at 6-inch intervals around the perimeter and at 12-inch intervals along the intermediate studs, spacing the panels $\frac{1}{8}$ inch apart and offsetting their edges from those of the sheathing panels by 16 inches.

A TRIO OF EARTHQUAKE VALVES

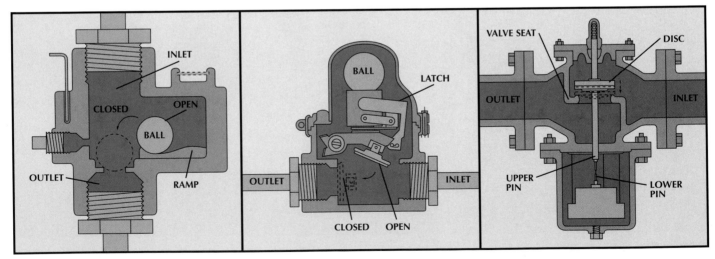

Three valves.

Designed for professional installation, earthquake valves come in a wide range of designs and prices. Simplest and least expensive is the valve at left, which consists of a metal ball perched on a ramp. When the valve is jolted by a tremor, the ball rolls off the ramp and over the gas line, stopping the flow of gas. In the more sensitive valve at center, a metal ball triggers a latch mechanism that clamps against the outlet end of the valve like a closing door. Most sophisticated is the valve at right, which bears the seal of approval of Underwriters Laboratories, the fire-protection organization whose recommendation is most widely accepted by fire-fighting agencies and insurance companies. In this valve, a pendulum-weighted lower pin supports an upper pin set into a disk. When an earthquake strikes, the pendulum holds the lower pin stationary; the upper pin, dislodged by the tremor, falls downward and the disk plugs the valve seat.

Violent winds can easily destroy a vacation home, literally ripping off the roof or tearing the walls loose from their foundation. If your cabin is in an area subject to hurricanes such as the Atlantic and Gulf coasts, you can take steps to anchor the structure. Check local building codes to see if reinforcement of your cabin is required.

Reinforcing the Structure: For a cabin built with stud walls, use special hardware to anchor the studs and soleplates to the foundation, the band and header joists to the sill plates, the walls to the band and

header joists, and the roof rafters to the studs *(below and page 92)*. If you plan to take such measures, build a block-wall foundation *(pages 24-33)*, embedding bolts for the anchor-downs that will adjoin door and window openings *(below)* long enough to pass through the subfloor and soleplates. Frame the walls as for a prefab cottage *(pages 36-43)*, but drill holes through the soleplates for the anchor bolts, and raise the walls and install the hardware before nailing the siding. Until the siding is in place, support the walls with diagonal bracing attached to stakes driven into the ground

(page 63, Step 4). An existing structure can also be reinforced *(page 92)*. Consult local codes or a building professional for the type and placement of hardware needed.

Additional Precautions: When a storm threatens, you can weight down the roof of your cabin with sandbags for extra protection. Also board up windows, leaving one or two slightly open on the lee—or sheltered—side of the house to equalize the air pressure inside and out. During a hurricane the higher air pressure indoors can burst doors and windows out of their frames.

 TOOLS

Socket wrench
Hammer
Keyhole saw

 **MATERIALS**

Anchor-downs and lag screws
Connector plates and nails
Strap ties and nails

Hurricane ties and nails
Silicone caulk
Rafter-to-stud connectors
  and nails
Wall-covering repair materials

 **SAFETY TIPS**

Goggles protect your eyes when you are hammering.

REINFORCING A CABIN

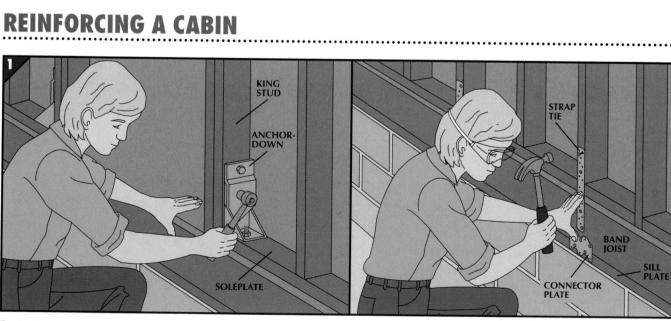

1. Anchoring the walls.
◆ On each side of door and window openings, use a socket wrench to fasten the horizontal flange of an anchor-down to the anchor bolt in the foundation. Bolt the vertical flange to the

outside of the king stud with the lag screws recommended by the manufacturer *(above, left)*.
◆ At every second stud, tie the band or header joist to the sill plate with a connector plate, fastened with the nails

recommended by the manufacturer, then fasten a strap tie across the seam between each stud and the band or header joist with the recommended nails, filling all the holes in the strap *(above, right)*.

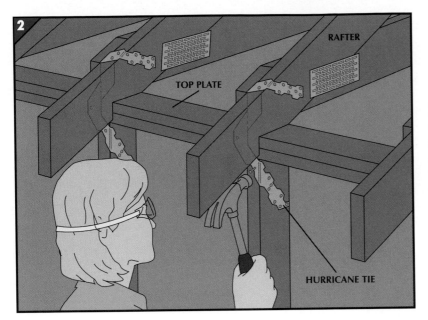

2. Strapping the roof to the wall.

◆ With the nails recommended by the anchor manufacturer, nail one flange of a hurricane tie to a rafter and the other to the top plate of the wall *(left)*.

◆ Repeat the procedure to install an anchor at every rafter.

MEASURES FOR EXISTING STRUCTURES

1. Anchoring floors and walls.

◆ At every second stud, align a strap tie vertically on the wall siding over the sill plate, band or header joist, soleplate, and stud.

◆ With the nails recommended by the manufacturer, fasten the tie to the wall, driving a nail into each hole in the strap *(right)*.

If the siding is uneven or angled, as with clapboard or vinyl siding, cut through it with a keyhole saw to make a recess for the strap, then nail the strap directly to the sheathing. Seal the cut with silicone caulking.

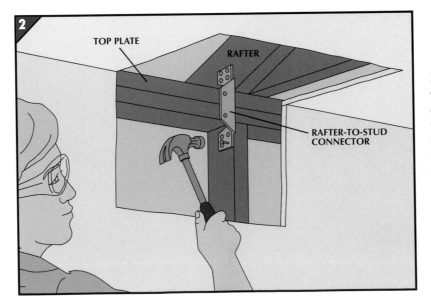

2. Linking walls and roof.

◆ Inside the cabin, remove sections of the wall covering with a keyhole saw to expose every second joint between the studs, top plate, and rafters.

◆ Nail one flange of a rafter-to-stud connector to the rafter and the other to the stud with the manufacturer's recommended nails *(left)*.

◆ Repair the wall covering.

The Lay of the Land: Clues to Foil a Flood

Water can be a threat to a country cabin. Rushing in a torrent, trickling down a slope, or rising from a flooded river, it can damage or destroy the sturdiest structure. To some extent you can meet the danger by using a special method of construction—building a cabin on a set of high poles, for example *(pages 16-19)*, may raise the structure above flood levels—but the real key to protecting a cabin from floods is the right choice of a building site.

Avoiding Troublespots: Sometimes the choice of site is fairly obvious. The closer a cabin is to a river or lake, the more likely it is to be damaged in a flood. Elsewhere, the problems of correct siting are relatively subtle, and locations that seem ideal at first glance may turn out to be the most vulnerable. A site next to a peaceful stream at the bottom of a ravine or valley, for example, may look safe, especially if you set your cabin well above the water level. Actually, it is a site to be avoided. During or after a heavy rain, the stream is likely to rise rapidly and flow with great force, destroying any property in its path. Other danger spots, along with the safest locations to build on them, are shown below and opposite.

Assessing a Site: A surveyor or landscape architect can identify potential flood problems for you, but you can do a good deal of preliminary detective work yourself. Start by asking neighbors and the area office of the Soil Conservation Service about the history of flooding at or near the site you are considering. Then study the site itself during a rainstorm. As the water runs off, you will see it flowing or collecting in natural drainage paths—areas that should not be blocked by any structure you build.

Vegetation and topographic features give additional clues to potential problems. Plants growing in a generally arid plot of ground indicate a spot that may become a short-lived pond or waterway during a heavy rain. Smooth, rounded boulders were probably shaped by water flowing over them repeatedly in the past. Level ground near creeks and streams is a likely sign of periodic flooding.

A steep ravine or valley.
The cabin in the background is sited much too close to a stream running along the bottom of a narrow ravine. In a storm, the volume and velocity of the stream will increase, and water will rise up the sides of the steep slope. The cabin in the forefront, situated on a gradual slope well away from the stream, is safe from such flash floods.

An upland meadow.

The cabin in the center of the picture is located in a depressed area that collects rainwater, and the driveway that links it to a main road cuts across the natural drainage path around the building site; in a storm, this roadway would channel water directly into the dishlike meadow. The cabin to the right is built on a higher site that drains quickly; its driveway follows the contour of the land, and underground culverts protect the driveway from a washout.

CULVERTS

Near a river.

The cabin in the foreground is built in the oxbow of a river, at the heart of a floodplain; in a heavy rain, the river might widen, completely submerging the site. The cabin in the distance, on a gentle slope well above the flood plain, lies clear of the probable flood pattern.

By a lake.

On lakefront property, it may be tempting to build a cabin or cottage with the closest and best possible view of the water. But sand is a highly unstable surface on which to build anything of substance. The cabin close to the lake shoreline is vulnerable to high winds and shifting sands. The cabin on the right is positioned safely on slightly elevated and solid ground.

Before constructing a cabin in snow country you must be sure that you will be able to reach it through deep snow, and that the structure will remain comfortable throughout a long, severe winter. Improve access to the cabin by building a raised boardwalk *(page 96)*; its sections can be separated and stored in the spring, then reassembled before the snow falls.

Locating the Cabin: Hilltops tend to be too windy for winter comfort; idyllic-looking "sheltered valleys" are generally reservoirs of deep snow and cold air. The best location for a cabin is on a south-facing slope, which gets light and warmth from the low winter sun. Fortunately, prevailing winter winds in most snowy parts of North America come from the north or northwest, so that setting your main door and windows toward the sun also keeps them on the downwind side. Do not place a building far from a plowed road unless you plan to get to it by snowshoe or with a snowmobile.

Cold-Climate Construction: Continuous masonry-block foundation walls *(pages 24-33)* are the warmest, and you can insulate them from the outside with packed snow; make sure the base of the foundation rests below the frost line. Insulate walls and install double-glazed glass for windows. Add to comfort and save on fuel costs by shielding the area outside the main door of the cabin with an enclosed entryway *(pages 97-99)* that can double as a woodshed.

The roof of a snow-country cabin may need thick rafters and special bracing to support the snow, or a steep pitch to shed snow *(page 96, chart)*. A roof steep enough to shed snow has an obvious advantage but it has disadvantages, too. It requires far more roofing material to cover a given floor area, and much of the high space underneath the rafters may be wasted. The rafters of a steep roof must be fastened securely to the wall *(page 92, Step 2)* to combat strong winds that would flow over a lower roof.

 TOOLS

Carpenter's level	Maul
Circular saw	Water level
Electric drill	Carpenter's square	Hacksaw
Socket wrench	Plumb bob	Mason's line
	Auger	Handsaw

 **MATERIALS**

1 x 2s, 1 x 4s, 1 x 6s
2 x 4s, 2 x 6s
Pressure-treated 2 x 8s, 2 x 10s
Exterior grade plywood ($\frac{3}{4}$")
Galvanized common nails (2", 3", $3\frac{1}{2}$")
Ring-shank nails ($2\frac{1}{2}$")
Lag screws ($\frac{1}{2}$" x 6")

Carriage bolts ($\frac{3}{8}$ x 5", 6")
Materials for concrete piers
Polyethylene sheeting (6-mil)
Joist hangers, multipurpose framing anchors, and nails
Concrete mix
Prefabricated stairs
Siding and roofing materials

 **SAFETY TIPS**

Wear safety goggles when hammering and when operating a power tool. Put on gloves to handle pressure-treated lumber; add a dust mask when cutting it.

A cabin ready for winter's worst.

Evergreen trees behind and beside the cabin at right act as windbreaks, but none are close enough to topple onto the roof. Trees have been cleared from the downwind, south side of the cabin to allow the sun to warm it; one deciduous tree remains, blocking little sun in winter but offering shade in summer. Similarly, the cabin's overhanging eaves block the rays of a high, hot summer sun but let in those of a low winter sun. The eaves are extended at one point to shelter an enclosed entryway and the steps leading up to it. A raised boardwalk, which can be dismantled in spring, leads from the front steps to the deck and on out to the driveway. A snow fence prevents blowing snow from drifting onto the cabin's driveway in the foreground.

RAFTERS FOR SNOW COUNTRY

Roof Slope	4" in 12"			7" in 12"			10" in 12"			14" in 12"		
Rafter Span	9'	12'	15'	9'	12'	15'	9'	12'	15'	9'	12'	15'
Snow Load 50 lbs.	2 x 6	2 x 8	2 x 10	2 x 6	2 x 8	2 x 10	2 x 6	2 x 8	2 x 10	2 x 6	2 x 8	2 x 8
60 lbs.	2 x 6	2 x 10	2 x 10	2 x 6	2 x 8	2 x 10	2 x 6	2 x 8	2 x 10	2 x 6	2 x 8	2 x 8
70 lbs	2 x 8	2 x 10	2 x 12	2 x 6	2 x 10	2 x 10	2 x 6	2 x 8	2 x 10	2 x 6	2 x 8	2 x 10

Picking the right size rafters.

The chart above lists the correct lumber sizes for rafters spaced 16 inches apart on a roof in a snowy region. To use the chart, find the vertical columns for your roof slope, then read down the column to the horizontal row for the rafter span and the snow load in your area. If the exact slope, span, and load for your cabin do not appear on the chart, use the next lower figure for slope, and the next higher for span and load. To get the figure for ground-snow load in your area, check with the local office of the Federal Housing Administration or an architect or structural engineer.

A roof for heavy snow.

The slope of the roof shown at right rises a steep 30 degrees, or 7 inches for every 12 inches of horizontal run, and is a prudent choice for snow country. If covered with metal roofing *(pages 64-65),* it will shed snow quickly. A roof of the same slope, covered with asphalt shingles, won't shed snow as well, and to keep melting snow from leaking through, would need flashing extending 8 to 10 inches above the line of the walls and lapped under the two lowest courses of shingles *(right).* Clear the roof after heavy snowfalls with a roof rake—a long-handled scraper available from hardware stores or homemade by nailing and bracing a 2-foot 1-by-6 to the end of a long pole.

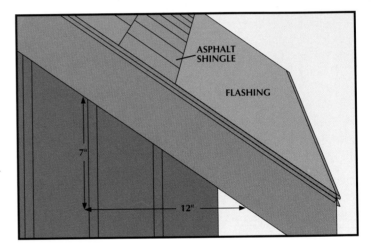

A path over snow and mud.

The sections of this raised boardwalk can be separated and stored in spring, then reassembled before the first heavy heavy snow. For the walkway, make open boxes of 2-by-6s, 6 feet long and 3 feet wide, with the long boards nailed to the ends of the shorter ones. Plank the tops of the boxes with 1-by-6s spaced $\frac{1}{4}$ inch apart. For each H-shaped support, use 6-foot 2-by-4 uprights 3 feet apart, and bolt a pair of 2-by-4 crosspieces between them $2\frac{1}{2}$ feet from the bottom. Nail 1-by-4 diagonal braces across the bottom half of the H. To assemble the sections, bolt the boxes together between the uprights, resting their bottoms on the crosspieces. Add handrails and 1-by-4 braces from one H to the next. Attach the end of the boardwalk to the cabin's entryway, and install a flight of steps at the other end.

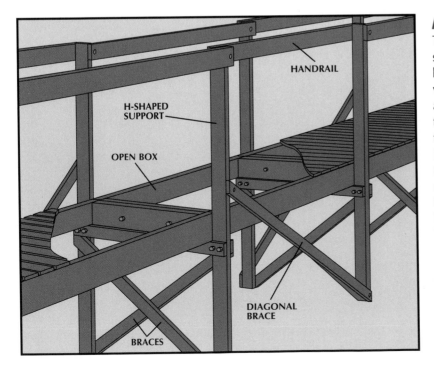

A DOORWAY SHELTERED FROM WIND AND SNOW

1. Extending the rafters.

◆ Miter one end of a 2-by-6 to an angle matching that of the roof slope.

◆ Starting at one side of the planned entryway, set the board alongside one of the main roof rafters with its mitered end up against the house wall and its top aligned with the top of the rafter.

◆ With a carpenter's level draw a vertical line on the 2-by-6 at the point where you plan to build the outside wall of the entryway *(right)*.

◆ Take the 2-by-6 down and draw a $3\frac{1}{2}$-inch line with a carpenter's square at a right angle from the first line to the bottom edge of the 2-by-6 *(inset)*.

◆ Cut the board at the lines with a circular saw and use it as a template to cut a 2-by-6 for each rafter that will extend over the entryway.

◆ At each end of the entryway, nail one of the boards onto a rafter with 3-inch galvanized common nails, driving two at both ends, then every 16 inches in between in a zigzag pattern.

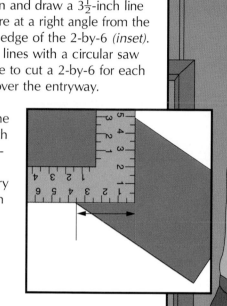

SHIM

STRUT

2. Bracing the extended rafters.

◆ Cut and position 1-by-2 horizontal struts on the house wall to brace the rafter extensions temporarily; if necessary, place shims between the ends of the struts and the wall to align the extensions perfectly with the existing rafters *(left)*.

◆ Hang a plumb bob from the end of one of the extensions to mark the outside edge of a foundation pier for the entryway. Mark the location of a second pier at the opposite end of the entryway; if the distance between the piers is greater than 10 feet, add a third pier in between.

◆ Cast footings for the piers at the same depth as the footings of the cabin and install two masonry piers *(pages 20-23)*.

◆ Assemble a girder from three pressure-treated 2-by-10s and install it atop the piers *(page 22, Step 5)*, aligning its ends flush with those of the piers.

3. Building the platform support.

◆ Make a plate to support the platform's joists at the doorway from a pressure-treated 2-by-8 cut a few inches longer than the desired length of the entryway platform.

◆ At the end of the joist plate opposite the proposed stairs, make a mark 1 inch from the end for the first joist, then continue marking the plate at 16-inch intervals for the rest of the joists.

◆ Tack a plumb bob to the outside face of the rafter extension where it meets the wall, and align the joist plate so the outside of the first joist mark is under the plumb bob and the plate's bottom edge is level with the top of the entryway girder. Have a helper mark the outline of the plate on the wall and door molding.

◆ Make marks above the joist plate on both sides of the door molding at a height that equals the thickness of the platform's decking, and cut off the bottom of the door molding at these marks.

◆ Fasten the joist plate to the wall with $\frac{1}{2}$- by-6-inch lag screws.

◆ Move the plumb bob to the end of the rafter extension, then using a carpenter's square, transfer the joist locations to the girder *(right)*.

JOIST PLATE

FIRST JOIST MARK

GIRDER

4. Hanging the joists.

◆ At the marks on the joist plate, nail joist hangers.

◆ Place pressure-treated 2-by-8 joists in the hangers, and set their opposite ends on the girder marks.

◆ Nail the joist hangers to the joists *(left)*. Attach the other end of the joists to the girder with multipurpose framing anchors.

◆ Add a platform of $\frac{3}{4}$-inch exterior-grade plywood, fastening it to the joists with $2\frac{1}{2}$-inch ring-shank nails *(page 33, Step 5)*; or fasten decking of pressure-treated 2-by-6s, separated by $\frac{1}{4}$ inch, with 3-inch common nails.

◆ Pour shallow concrete footings and fasten a set of prefabricated steps to the end joist with framing anchors *(page 52, Step 4)*.

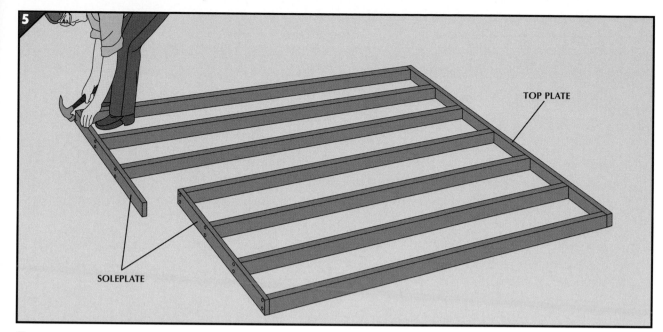

TOP PLATE

SOLEPLATE

5. Framing the outside wall.

◆ Cut two 2-by-4s to the length of the outside wall for a top and soleplate and mark them for studs to align with the rafter extensions.

◆ Because the soleplate will rest on both the entryway floor and on the girder, the studs will be of unequal lengths: Cut the plate to the length of the floor and cut studs to fit between the top plate and the two sections of soleplate when the wall is fastened to the rafter extensions.

◆ Attach the studs to the top plate and the soleplate sections with $3\frac{1}{2}$-inch common nails (above).

◆ With a helper, lift the frame into position. Nail the soleplate to the girder and toenail it through the entryway floor into the joists.

◆ Toenail the rafter extensions to the top plate, then remove the struts.

◆ Install the remaining rafter extensions (page 97, Step 1) and toenail them to the top plate.

6. Framing the end walls.

◆ Cut a soleplate for the end wall of the entryway and nail it to the floor.

◆ Hold a stud against the end rafter extension and mark it to create a $1\frac{1}{2}$-inch-deep notch (right and inset).

◆ Mark other studs in the same way 16 inches apart to complete the wall.

◆ Cut the studs at the marks and attach each one to the rafter with two 3-inch galvanized common nails.

◆ Install siding over the stud walls and extend the roofing, slipping the new roofing under the existing layer.

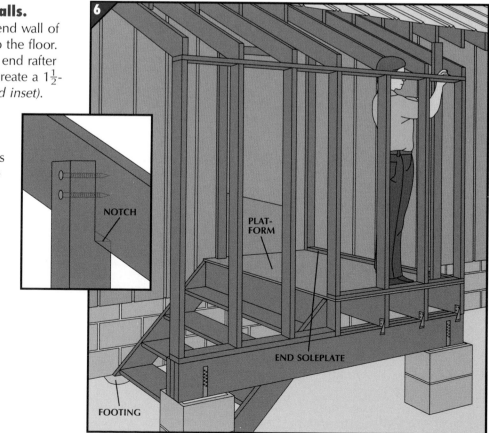

NOTCH

PLAT-FORM

END SOLEPLATE

FOOTING

Adding the Amenities

Just because you are getting away from it all doesn't mean that you have to give up comfort, even when your cabin or cottage is not equipped with all the conveniences that you take for granted at home. Most of the basic necessities—water, heat, and waste disposal—can still be made available with a minimum of time and expense.

Priming a pump →

Bringing running water to a cabin may simply involve hooking up to a public water line, but if you are off the beaten path, far from public utilities, you will need to tap a supply of surface, rain, or ground water. Before you do so, have the water analyzed by the local health department.

Aboveground Sources: Surface water from a stream or lake is the easiest to tap *(below)*. Rain water can be collected by means of a catchment system that runs the water to a holding tank, or cistern *(pages 103-105)*, to be pumped out as needed. A 275-gallon cistern—a galvanized-steel pressure tank sold by plumbing suppliers—holds enough water for weekend use by a family of six.

Going Underground: Digging a well will nearly always ensure a regular water supply. At a site on sandy soil, ground water can usually be tapped easily. Check with neighbors; if their experience indicates that ground water in the area is within 30 feet of the surface, you can drive a well by hand *(pages 105-106)*. In a soil so dense or rocky that you cannot drive a pipe, consider an old-fashioned dug well. Hire a professional to dig the shaft with a backhoe and line it with a ceramic casing. You can then install a jet pump *(pages 108-109)* to bring up the water that collects at the bottom.

Where water is below 30 feet of the surface in any kind of soil, most people turn to a professional well driller, whose equipment can go as deep as necessary to reach water, and who can also install and seal a galvanized-steel casing. From that point, you can lower an electric pump into the well *(pages 110-114)* and hook it up yourself.

TOOLS

Screwdriver	Keyhole saw	Pipe wrenches
Electric drill	Hammer	Shovel
Hole saw ($1\frac{3}{4}$")	Tin snips	Sledgehammer
Circular saw	Hand stapler	

MATERIALS

Polyethylene pipe (1")	PVC primer and cement
Adapters, bushings	Plywood ($\frac{1}{2}$")
Hose clamps	1 x 4s
Plumbing-sealant tape	Galvanized common
Intake screen (1")	nails ($1\frac{1}{2}$")
Concrete block	Galvanized hardware
Nylon cord	cloth ($\frac{1}{4}$" holes)
Roof gutters and downspout	Cistern, nipple, and
Gutter guards	vent cap
Plastic garbage can	Pump
(30-gallon)	Galvanized steel pipe
Silicone sealant	and fittings ($1\frac{1}{4}$")
PVC adapters and	Drive point shaft
bushings ($1\frac{1}{4}$", $1\frac{1}{2}$")	Drive cap

SAFETY TIPS

Protect your eyes with goggles when operating a power tool or when driving steel pipe into the ground.

AN INTAKE FOR SURFACE WATER

1. Assembling the pipe intake.
◆ Run 1-inch flexible polyethylene pipe from the surface water source to the cabin.
◆ Slide a hose clamp over the intake end of the pipe, insert a 1-inch polyvinyl chloride (PVC) pipe adapter with male threads *(right)*, then secure the adapter by tightening the hose clamp.
◆ Beginning at the outer end of the adapter, wrap plumbing-sealant tape around the threads, following the direction of the threads, then screw on a 1-inch intake screen.

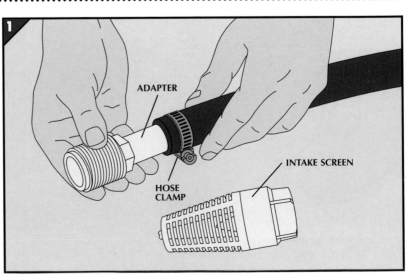

ADAPTER

HOSE CLAMP

INTAKE SCREEN

2. Positioning the pipe.

◆ Run the intake end of the pipe through the core of a concrete block.

◆ Tie a length of nylon cord to the intake screen and place the block on the river or lake bottom as far from shore as you can safely wade. Tie the other end of the nylon cord to a float such as a stoppered plastic jug to hold the intake at least 2 feet above the bottom (left). If the bottom of the lake or river drops off immediately, go out in a rowboat, tie a long cord to the pipe, and drop the pipe and block into the water. Tie the cord to a jug.

◆ Using an adapter, hook up the free end of the pipe to a tap if the cabin is downhill from the source. If the cabin is uphill, hook it to a pump (pages 107-109).

A CATCHMENT FOR RAINWATER

1. Attaching gutter guards.

◆ Clean the roof gutters—or install gutters if none exist.

◆ Add a downspout—or shorten an existing one—ending it about 3 feet above the ground.

◆ Shield the gutter from leaves and other debris with gutter guards—5-foot lengths of plastic screening—cutting and bending the pieces so that they fit snugly at the sides and around the gutter's braces (right).

GUTTER GUARD

2. Connecting the pipe.

◆ With a drill fitted with a $1\frac{3}{4}$-inch hole saw, cut an opening 10 inches from the top of a collector drum—a new 30-gallon plastic garbage can.

◆ Spread silicone sealant on the threads of a $1\frac{1}{2}$-inch PVC sink-drain adapter and insert it into the hole and secure it with its nut *(left)*.

◆ To connect the unthreaded outer end of this adapter to your plastic pipe, as shown in the inset, fasten a $1\frac{1}{2}$-inch cleanout fitting to the drain adapter with PVC cement, screw a $1\frac{1}{2}$-inch-to-$1\frac{1}{4}$-inch reducer bushing to the cleanout fitting, and a $1\frac{1}{4}$-inch male adapter to the reducer bushing.

◆ Run 1-inch flexible polyethylene pipe to the cistern and attach it to the male adapter with a hose clamp.

◆ Drill a $\frac{1}{8}$-inch hole 1 to 3 inches from the bottom of the drum to allow water to drain between rains to prevent stagnation.

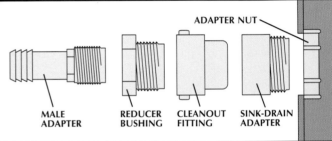

MALE ADAPTER | REDUCER BUSHING | CLEANOUT FITTING | SINK-DRAIN ADAPTER | ADAPTER NUT

3. Assembling the elements.

◆ Place the collector drum directly under the shortened downspout.

◆ To make a trough to break the force of the water, first cut a square of $\frac{1}{2}$-inch plywood with sides as long as the drum's outside diameter, and cut a 4-inch hole in its center with a keyhole saw. Fasten 1-by-4s to its sides with $1\frac{1}{2}$-inch galvanized common nails to form a box *(right)*.

◆ With tin snips, cut a piece of galvanized hardware cloth with $\frac{1}{4}$-inch holes to the size of the trough. Turn the box over and staple the hardware cloth to the top of the 1-by-4s.

◆ Position the trough centered over the top of the drum.

◆ Place a cistern as close as possible to the cabin, but downhill so its top is below the level of the outlet on the collector drum. If necessary, raise the drum on a platform or dig a pit for the cistern.

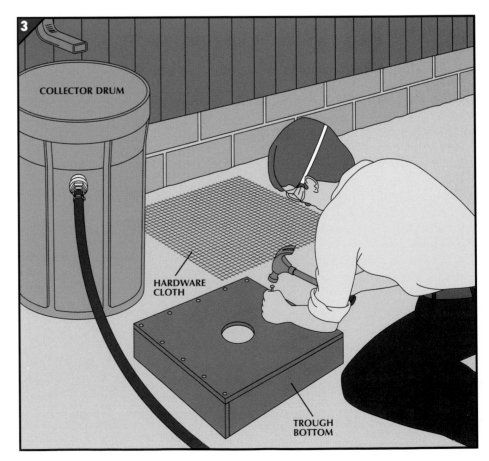

COLLECTOR DRUM

HARDWARE CLOTH

TROUGH BOTTOM

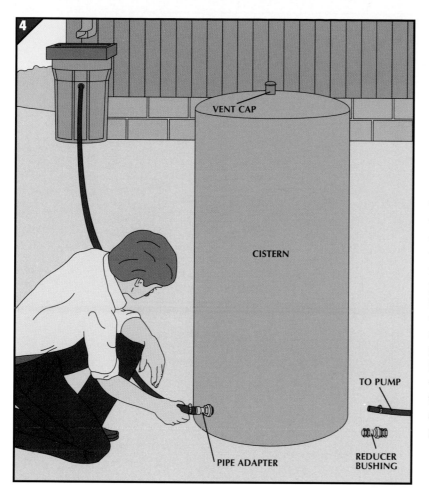

4. Connecting the cistern.

◆ Remove the threaded plug on top of the cistern and replace it with a nipple—a 6-inch length of $1\frac{1}{2}$-inch pipe with male threads at each end. Screw on a $1\frac{1}{2}$-inch vent cap—a mushroom-shaped fitting with holes to let the air out of the tank as it fills.
◆ Install a $1\frac{1}{4}$-inch pipe adapter in the opening near the bottom of the cistern.
◆ Slip a hose clamp over the pipe from the collector drum and push the pipe onto the adapter *(left)*. Tighten the hose clamp.
◆ Insert a $1\frac{1}{4}$-to-1-inch threaded reducer bushing into the opening near the bottom of the tank opposite the intake from the drum.
◆ Run another length of pipe from the reducer bushing to the cabin to an indoor pump—for a cistern, a lift pump or a jet pump is suitable *(pages 107-109)*.

DRIVING A WELL

1. Attaching a drive-point shaft.

◆ With two pipe wrenches, fasten a coupling—a short length of pipe with female threads at both ends—between a 4-foot section of $1\frac{1}{4}$-inch galvanized steel pipe and a drive-point shaft—a special section of pipe with screened openings and a sharp point at one end *(right)*.
◆ Screw a drive cap—a piece that covers and protects the pipe threads—to the other end of the pipe.
◆ Dig a starter hole 2 feet deep at the desired location for the well.
◆ Push the drive point into the hole.

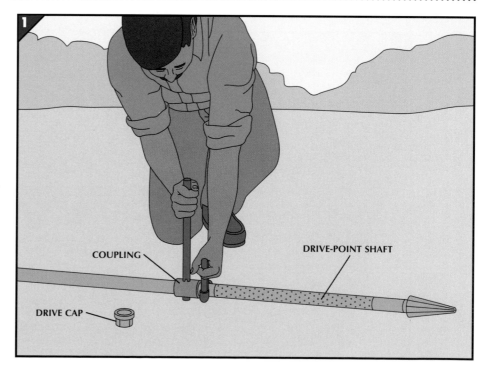

2. Sinking pipe sections.

◆ Drive the assembly about 1 foot into the ground with a sledgehammer *(right)* or with a heavy-duty steel post pounder *(photograph)*; if the pipe starts to angle, tap it sideways to right it.

◆ Retighten the coupling around the pipe and drive-point shaft, then continue driving the assembly. When it is almost at ground level, remove the drive cap and add another section of pipe with a coupling as in Step 1.

◆ Continue driving the assembly into the ground and retightening the coupling in the same way; each time you remove the drive cap to add a section of pipe, lower a string with a nut attached to the end inside the pipe to test for water. When you hear a splash, you have reached water; drive the pipe 2 feet deeper at this point.

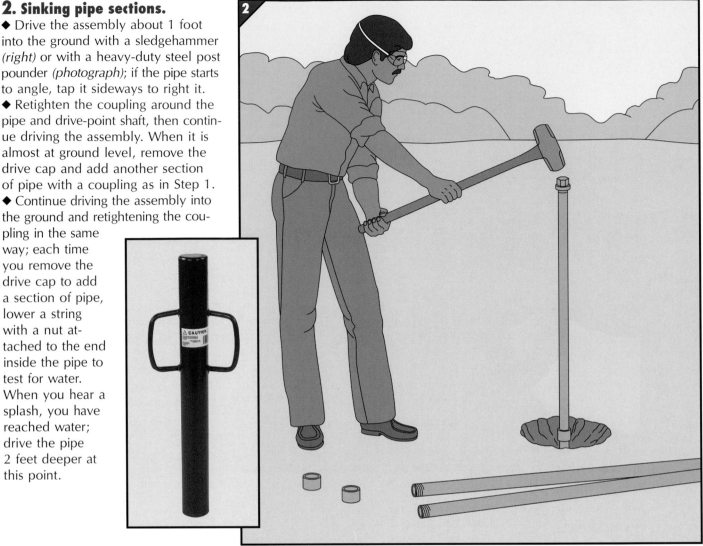

3. Capping the well pipe.

◆ Remove the drive cap and thread a $1\frac{1}{4}$-inch steel T-fitting with a 1-inch side outlet to the pipe *(left)*.

◆ Tighten the fitting with a pipe wrench and close off the top with a $1\frac{1}{4}$-inch threaded plug.

◆ Screw a 1-inch plastic pipe adapter to the side outlet, clamp 1-inch flexible polyethylene pipe to it and run the pipe to your pump.

If the flow of water is insufficient when you use the pump, the drive point screen may be clogged. To clear it, use the pump briefly and remove the plug from the top of the T-fitting—the water will fall back down the well pipe and force sand and sediment away from the screen. Repeat this procedure until water flows freely.

T-FITTING

Depending on the source of water and the power available, your choice of pumps ranges from an old-fashioned hand-operated lift pump to more modern electric jet and submersible models.

Hand Power: The least expensive and most easily installed pump is the lift pump *(below)*, available at most farm-equipment supply stores, but this type of pump works only if the water level is less than 25 feet lower than the pump. It consists of an iron cylinder fitted with a leather-rimmed piston, a handle to move the piston, and a pipe running from the cylinder to the water supply.

Electric Pumps: Power-operated pumps will raise water any distance.

The one most often used for surface-water sources is the jet pump *(pages 108-109)*, which pulls the water to a pressure tank. The best power pump for deep drilled wells is the submersible type *(pages 110-114)*, which pushes water up to the tank.

If you cannot plug into utility power at or near your building site, you will need a generator *(page 8)* supplying 4,000 watts or more to power a jet or submersible pump.

Shutting Down for the Winter: If you do not plan to use your cabin in winter, open all of the valves and draincocks in your water system—disassembling pipes if necessary—to let water out and air into parts of the system that will be exposed to freezing temperatures.

 TOOLS

Keyhole saw
Screwdriver
Cable ripper
Wire strippers
Wrench

 **MATERIALS**

Lift pump
Flexible polyethylene pipe ($\frac{3}{4}$", 1", $1\frac{1}{4}$")
Bushings
Adapters
Hose clamps
Ejector unit, nipple, check valve

Jet pump
Pressure tank and fittings
Drain, gate, and pressure-relief valves
Electric cable (14-gauge)
Plumbing-sealant tape

INSTALLING A LIFT PUMP

Mounting the pump indoors.

◆ With a keyhole saw, cut a 2-inch hole in the counter next to your sink.
◆ Run 1-inch flexible polyethylene pipe from the water source up through the hole.
◆ Thread a $1\frac{1}{4}$-to-1-inch reducer bushing into the $1\frac{1}{4}$-inch fitting at the bottom of the pump, then screw on a 1-inch male adapter.
◆ Slide a hose clamp over the pipe, push the pipe over the adapter *(right)*, and tighten the hose clamp.
◆ Screw the pump to the countertop.

Before you work the pump handle to draw water, pour a cup of water into the top of the pump to wet the leather seals inside.

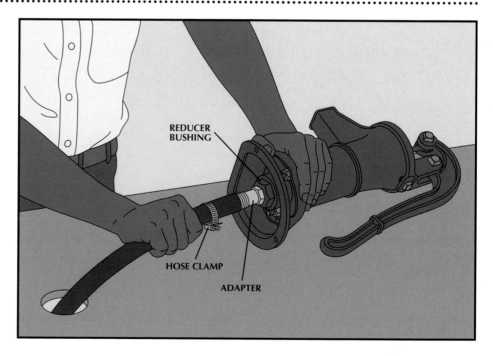

REDUCER BUSHING

HOSE CLAMP

ADAPTER

A JET PUMP

A typical installation.

In the system at right, an electric pump in a sheltered part of the cabin draws water up an intake pipe, through an ejector unit near the source of surface water, and up a flexible polyethylene suction pipe. Some of the water returns to the ejector through the pressure pipe; this water squirts through a nozzle in the unit, expands in a flared tube and creates a partial vacuum that can help suck water up to the pump from depths as great as 240 feet.

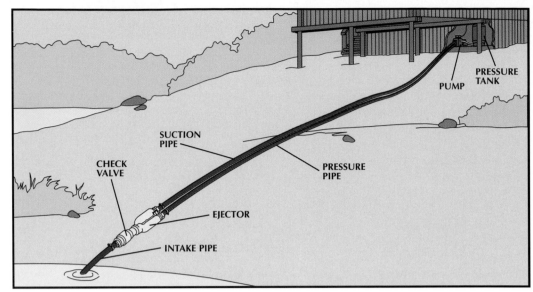

At the pump, the water that is not returned to the ejector flows through an outlet pipe to a pressure tank, from which it is drawn for use in the cabin. As the tank empties, its pressure drops; when it falls to a predetermined point, a pressure switch mounted on the pump closes to run the pump until the pressure is restored. When the pump is not running, a check valve located between the intake pipe and the ejector unit closes to keep the water trapped in the system.

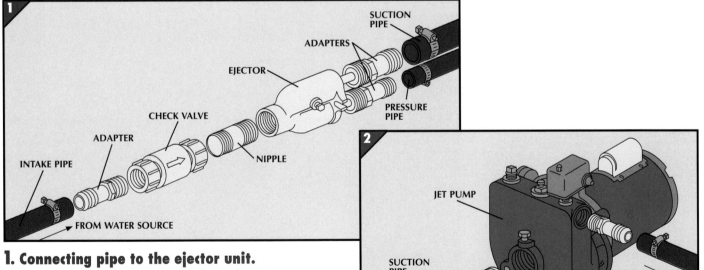

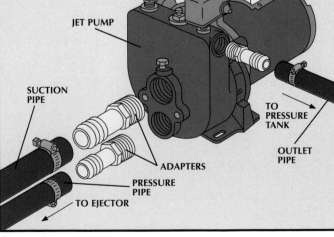

1. Connecting pipe to the ejector unit.

◆ Screw a nipple—a short piece of 1-inch pipe, threaded at both ends—into the single-ended intake of the ejector, then screw the check valve onto the nipple with the valve's flow-direction arrow pointing toward the ejector.
◆ Screw an adapter into the other end of the check valve, slide a hose clamp over the flexible polyethylene intake pipe, insert the adapter into the pipe and tighten the hose clamp.
◆ At the double-ended opening of the ejector, install adapters and hose clamps in the same way to hook up a 1¼-inch suction pipe and a 1-inch pressure pipe. (Larger pipes may be necessary for runs of more than 35 feet in length that need to raise water vertically more than 25 feet; consult the pump manufacturer.)

2. Hooking up the pump.

◆ Join the pressure and suction pipes to the matching openings on the pump with adapters and hose clamps.
◆ Attach ¾-inch flexible polyethylene pipe to the pressure tank outlet with an adapter and hose clamp and run this hose to the pressure tank.

3. Joining the pressure-tank fittings.

◆ Begin the connections at the tank by screwing a special four-arm T-assembly, available from the pressure-tank dealer, into the threaded opening at the base of the tank.

◆ Screw a standard T-fitting onto one side of the assembly and screw a drain valve into the top of the T-fitting.

◆ Install a 1-inch nipple to the other end of the T-fitting and then a gate valve, to control the flow of water to the cabin.

◆ Screw a pressure-relief valve into the middle of the four-arm T to bleed excess pressure from the tank.

◆ To link the tank with the jet pump, seal the two small openings at the top of the four-arm T with pipe plugs and fit the remaining opening with a 1-inch coupling and a 1-to-$\frac{3}{4}$-inch reducer bushing. Connect the bushing to the pump line with an adapter and a hose clamp.

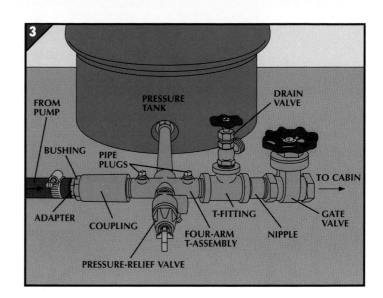

4. Wiring the pressure switch.

◆ Stretch 14-gauge cable from a power source to the terminals of the pressure switch, clamp the cable to the pump, but do not hook the other end to the power source.

◆ Screw the power wires—black and white in a 120-volt cable, black and either white or red in a 240-volt cable—to the outside switch terminals marked "Line" (left).

◆ Attach the copper or green ground wire to the grounding screw.

◆ Have an electrician hook up the pump wires to the service panel or generator.

5. Priming the pump.

◆ Open the drain valve at the pressure tank.

◆ Remove the plug from the pump's priming port, then loosen the lock nut and tighten the stem of the water-pressure control valve (right).

◆ Pour water into the priming port until the pump is completely full, then wrap the threads of the port plug with plumbing-sealant tape and screw it loosely in place.

◆ Turn on the pump. When air bubbles stop popping from the port, tighten the plug and loosen the valve stem until the needle on the pressure gauge is at the mark specified by the manufacturer.

◆ Tighten the lock nut.

◆ Close the pressure tank's drain valve.

On models with a hex-head bolt to regulate the water pressure, turn the bolt according to the manufacturer's instructions to set the control valve.

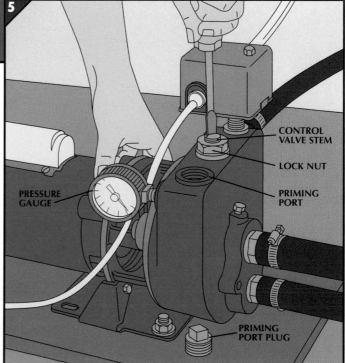

A Submersible Pump for a Drilled Well

Originally developed for mines and oil wells, the submersible pump has become the type most widely used in private water systems. It is silent, invisible, and virtually maintenance free.

Picking the Pieces: The professional who drills your well and installs its steel casing will recommend the size of pump you need; parts for the installation are available from pump dealers and plumbing suppliers. If your well is less than 400 feet deep, you can install the pump yourself by attaching it to flexible polyethylene pipe—ask the well driller to specify the length and grade of the pipe. Wells deeper than 400 feet require the pump to be fitted with heavy sections of galvanized-steel pipe—a job best left to the driller.

> ⚠️ **CAUTION** Seal off the well hole after drilling it until you are to install the pump. Turn power off at the source before connecting the pump wires.

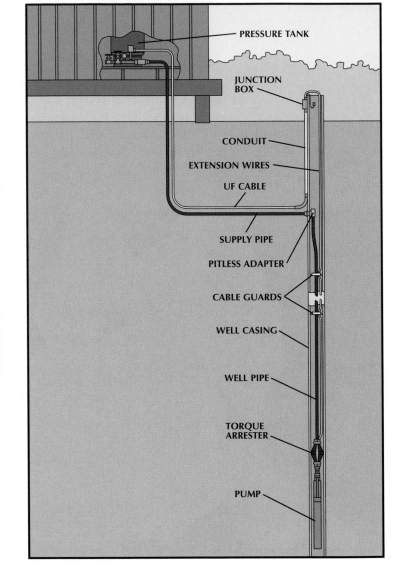

TOOLS

Shovel	Pipe wrench
Electric drill	Multipurpose
Hole saw	electrician's tool
Screwdriver	Wrench

MATERIALS

PLUMBING	WIRING
Submersible pump	Cable guards
Pitless adapter	Electrician's tape
Plastic pipe	Waterproof wires
Plastic T-fitting	Heat-shrink splice kit
Polyethylene pipe	Plastic conduit
Adapters	PVC primer and cement
Hose clamps	C-body
Torque arrester	UF cable
Well cap	Aluminum grounding block
Pressure tank	Wire caps
Check valve	Jumper wire
Pressure gauge	Pressure switch

Anatomy of a submersible pump.

Hung from a well pipe into the water of a drilled well, this submersible pump has a flexible torque arrester just above it that fits tightly against the well casing to keep the pipe from moving when the pump starts. The pipe itself is attached to an opening in the casing with a fitting called a pitless adapter, which seals the opening around the pipe. From this point, water flows through a supply pipe to a pressure tank.

Two waterproof extension wires and a ground wire, threaded through disks called cable guards, run up from the pump alongside the well pipe. At the top of the casing, these wires enter into an electrical junction box, where they are spliced to the wires of UF cable, designed for burial beneath the ground. The UF cable runs through a length of plastic conduit down the outside of the casing, then goes underground, in the same trench as the supply pipe, to a pressure switch mounted on the pressure tank.

INSTALLING THE SYSTEM

1. Attaching the pitless adapter to the casing.

◆ Dig a trench to a depth just below the frost line from the house to the well casing.

◆ Fit a drill with a steel-cutting hole saw of the same diameter as the nipple of the pitless adapter, and drill a hole into the well casing a few inches from the bottom of the trench.

◆ Partially assemble the pitless adapter and the handle for lowering it into the casing as shown in the inset: Slip the bracket's inner gasket over the threaded nipple; leave the outer gasket, retainer, and nut for later. Make a T-shaped handle from sections of plastic pipe secured by a T-fitting and with a threaded adapter on the end. Screw the handle into the top end of the pitless adapter.

◆ Slip the bracket onto the slider plate and lower the assembly into the casing until the nipple reaches the drilled hole.

◆ Have a helper in the trench pull the nipple through the hole and fasten it to the casing with the outer gasket, retainer ring, and nut (right).

◆ Raise the handle, disengaging the slider plate from the bracket, and pull it out of the casing.

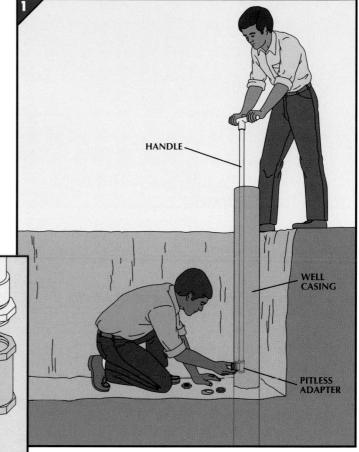

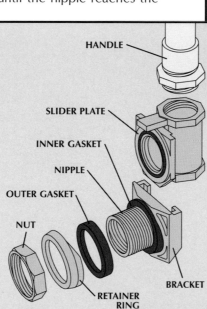

HANDLE

WELL CASING

PITLESS ADAPTER

HANDLE

SLIDER PLATE

INNER GASKET

NIPPLE

OUTER GASKET

NUT

RETAINER RING

BRACKET

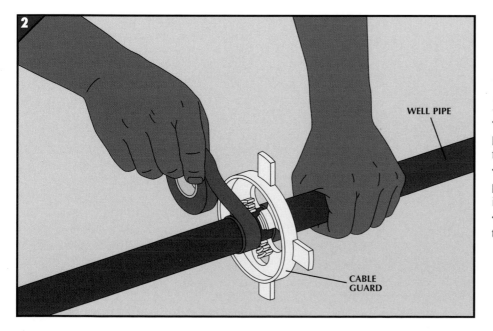

WELL PIPE

CABLE GUARD

2. Attaching the cable guards.

◆ Slide a cable guard onto the flexible polyethylene well pipe so it is 5 feet from the bottom.

◆ Wrap electrician's tape around the pipe on each side of the guard to keep it from slipping (left).

◆ Secure a guard every 15 feet along the pipe in the same way.

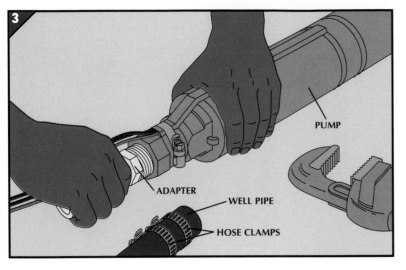

3. Linking the pipe and pump.
◆ Slide a pair of hose clamps onto the bottom of the well pipe and screw a flexible pipe adapter into the opening at the top of the pump *(left)*. Tighten the adapter with a pipe wrench.
◆ Fit the pipe onto the adapter and tighten the hose clamps.

4. Joining the pipe and adapter.
◆ Screw a plastic adapter to the end of the pitless adapter that is opposite the handle.
◆ Attach the well pipe to the adapter with two hose clamps *(right)*.
◆ Temporarily seal the opening in the slider plate with tape.

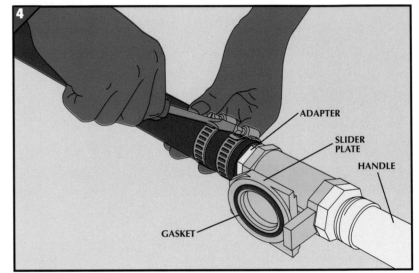

5. Extending the pump wires.
◆ Cut a pair of submersible extension wires and a ground wire 10 feet longer than the well pipe.
◆ Starting at the pump, run the wires along the pipe, threading them through the cable guards and leaving the extra wire at the top.
◆ Slide a length of shrink tubing—a rubber cylinder used to protect a splice—onto each pump wire, then slide a metal crimp connector over each extension wire.
◆ Strip $\frac{1}{2}$ inch of insulation from the ends of the wires, then twist the extension wires and ground wire to the pump wires.
◆ Place the crimp connectors over the wire splices and crush the connectors with an electrician's multipurpose tool *(left)*.
◆ Slide the tubing over the splices, then heat each length with the flame from a match or lighter until it shrinks around the connector, creating a watertight seal.

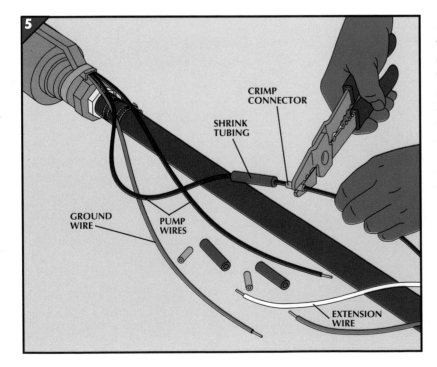

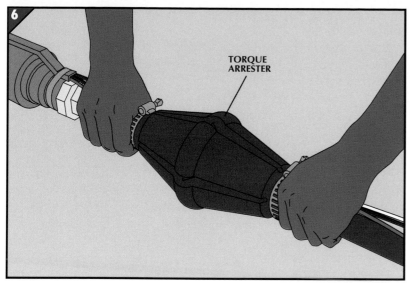

TORQUE ARRESTER

6. Installing the torque arrester.

◆ Loosely clamp the halves of a rubber torque arrester around the well pipe just above the pump.

◆ Push the ends of the arrester together, expanding the middle until it matches the inside diameter of the well casing *(left)*.

◆ Hold the arrester in position while a helper tightens the clamps.

7. Lowering the pump.

◆ Pad the rim of the well casing with rags to protect the pump extension wires.

◆ Working with a helper, lower the pump into the casing *(above)*.

◆ When the pitless adapter is near the casing, remove the tape from its slider plate and grease the rubber gasket of the plate with the lubricant supplied by the manufacturer.

◆ With the handle, guide the plate into the bracket section of the adapter, then unscrew the handle from the adapter.

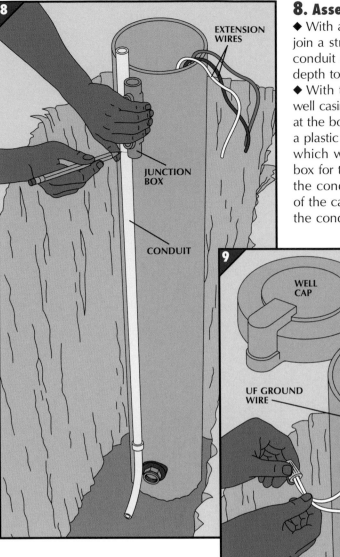

8. Assembling the conduit.

◆ With a coupling and cement, join a straight length of PVC conduit as long as the trench depth to a short curved section.

◆ With the conduit against the well casing so the curved section is at the bottom of the trench, hold a plastic fitting called a C-body—which will serve as a junction box for the pump wiring—beside the conduit just below the top of the casing. Mark the bottom of the conduit about 1 inch above the bottom the junction box *(left)*, cut the conduit at the mark, and attach the junction box to it.

◆ Run UF cable along the trench from the pressure switch, through the conduit, and into the junction box. Push the ends of the extension wires into the box.

◆ Drill a $\frac{1}{4}$-inch hole into the well casing near the junction box, 2 inches from the top, then attach an aluminum grounding block to the inside of the casing with a nut and bolt.

9. Connections at the wellhead.

◆ Strip 8 inches of plastic sheathing from each end of the UF cable.

◆ At the junction box, feed the cable's bare ground wire out through the top of the box and fasten it to the setscrew of the grounding block.

◆ With wire caps, join the cable wires to the extension wires, black to black and white to white *(left)*. Attach the extension ground wire to the grounding block setscrew.

◆ Screw on the junction box cover and seal the well with a cap that fits over the casing and junction box, holding the box against the casing.

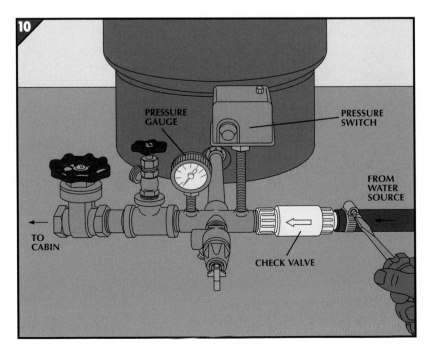

10. Connecting the supply pipe.

◆ Cut a length of polyethylene pipe to run along the trench from the pitless adapter nipple to the pressure tank.

◆ Screw an adapter to the nipple and attach the pipe to the nipple with a hose clamp.

◆ Secure the pipe to the pressure tank *(left)* as for a jet pump *(page 109)*, but substitute a check valve *(page 108)* for the 1-inch coupling, and install a pressure gauge and a pressure switch in the small openings on the T-assembly.

◆ At the pressure switch, connect the black and white cable wires to the inside switch terminals marked "Load." Connect the wires from your power source as for a jet pump *(page 109, Step 4)*, but the leave the ground wire free. With a wire cap, join ground wires of the power source to a short jumper wire, then connect the jumper to the switch grounding screw.

◆ Fill the trench wih earth.

Putting in an All-Purpose Sink

Even in the simplest of vacation cabins, a sink with running water is considered a basic amenity. As long as you have a supply of water—whether it is delivered by an electric pump or a hand-operated pitcher pump mounted indoors—a sink is an easily added convenience.

Choosing a Sink: The simplest sink to set up is an inexpensive plastic laundry tub, which has the added advantage of large size. However, if your pump is hand operated, you will need a surface on which to mount it; in that case, a better choice for a sink is a stainless-steel one designed to be set into a ready-made counter or a plywood shelf.

Making Connections: Flexible polyethylene pipe brings the water supply to either a pump or a faucet. Waste runs out through rigid plastic traps and T-fittings into a drain line of rigid plastic pipe leading to a drainage system.

Dealing with Waste: The waste from a sink—called gray water—generally contains such contaminants as soapsuds and food particles, so it should at least be drained to a pit *(pages 118-119)*; but many codes require a complete septic system *(pages 120-121)*.

 TOOLS

Screwdriver
Pipe wrench

 **MATERIALS**

Plumbing-sealant tape

Plumber's putty
Faucet assembly
Polyethylene pipe
Adapter

Hose clamp
Sink
Trap-and-drain assembly

 **SAFETY TIPS**

Wear rubber gloves when applying silicone sealant.

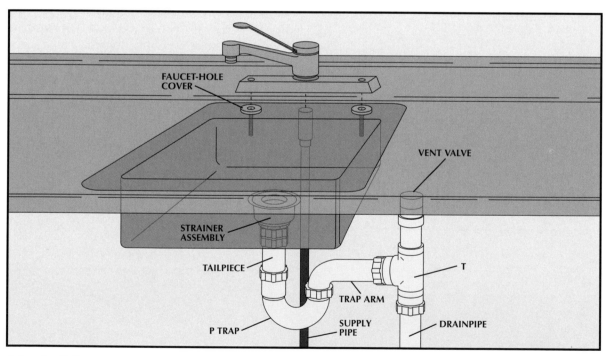

A basic sink.

In this installation, a standard kitchen sink is mounted in a hole cut through a ready-made counter. Water from an electric pump comes through a plastic supply pipe to a faucet attached to the middle hole of the sink; the outer holes are capped with faucet-hole covers, available from a plumbing supplier. For drainage, the sink is fitted with a strainer assembly, a tailpiece, and a P trap; from the trap, the waste is routed to the drainpipe through a trap arm and a T-fitting. A special in-house vent valve, permissible in many areas in place of a through-the-roof vent, is attached to the top of the T.

For a hand-operated pump, the faucet is omitted and all three holes in the sink are capped. The pump is mounted on the counter so it can empty into the sink *(page 107)*.

1. Connecting the faucet to the water supply.

◆ Wrap plumbing-sealant tape around all of the male threads of the connections between the faucet and the supply pipe.

◆ Apply plumber's putty to the underside of the faucet base.

◆ Fasten the faucet in the sink hole with the O-ring and nut.

◆ Screw on the steel coupling and attach the flexible-pipe adapter to the coupling.

◆ Mount the sink and slide the flexible polyethylene supply pipe over the adapter and secure the pipe with a hose clamp.

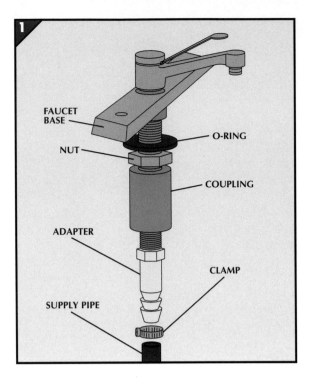

FAUCET BASE · O-RING · NUT · COUPLING · ADAPTER · CLAMP · SUPPLY PIPE

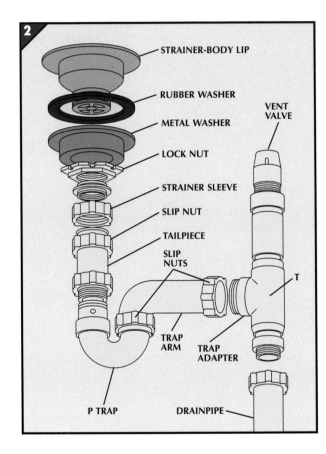

STRAINER-BODY LIP · RUBBER WASHER · METAL WASHER · LOCK NUT · STRAINER SLEEVE · SLIP NUT · TAILPIECE · SLIP NUTS · TRAP ARM · TRAP ADAPTER · P TRAP · DRAINPIPE · VENT VALVE · T

2. Installing the drain.

◆ Apply plumber's putty to the underside of the strainer-body lip and insert the strainer body in the sink's drain hole.

◆ Slip on the rubber and metal washers and secure them with the lock nut.

◆ Assemble the strainer sleeve, slip nut, and tailpiece and connect the tailpiece to the strainer body.

◆ Fasten the P trap to the tailpiece with a slip nut and washer. Connect the trap to the T with a short piece of pipe—called a trap arm.

◆ Attach a 4-inch pipe to the top of the T, then screw on a female-threaded adapter. Coat the threads of a vent valve with petroleum jelly to ensure an airtight fit, and screw the vent into the adapter.

◆ Slip a male adapter into the bottom of the T, slide the main drainpipe over the adapter, and fasten it with a slip nut.

◆ Attach the other end of the main drainpipe to the cabin's waste-disposal system *(pages 118-121)*.

TRICKS OF THE TRADE

Preventing Leaks with Sealant

To avoid leaks at slip joints, run a bead of silicone sealant around the inside faces of all slip nuts. Spread the sealant on the threads with a finger before installing the nut and closing off joints. In the drain assembly shown above, slip joints occur between the tailpiece and strainer sleeve, the P trap and trap arm, between the trap arm and trap adapter, and between the trap adapter and drain pipe.

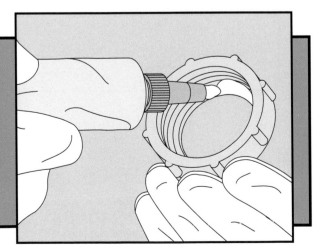

Dealing with human waste in areas not served by traditional plumbing and sewer systems can be problematic. Septic systems are a common option *(page 120)*, but they are sometimes prohibited in areas near lakes, rivers, and water supplies, or in regions with poor soil conditions. There are two environmentally friendly waste-treatment systems that do not require a septic system *(below)*: portable chemical toilets and composting toilet systems.

Chemical Toilets: Used by boaters and in recreational vehicles, chemical toilets are a practical option for the weekend cottager. Available in several sizes, a typical unit can be used by up to six people over a three-day period. When it has been filled to capacity—most models have a capacity indicator—the tank must be carried off and emptied into a pump-out service tank before being cleaned and reused.

Composting Waste: For a more permanent solution, consider installing a composting toilet. With these units, kitchen and garden scraps can be added to the human wastes for disposal. The materials decompose and can then be recycled into the soil. The styles range from small, self-contained units that need frequent maintenance to larger, more complex models with great capacity. Though some types use no water, others need to be connected to the water supply system. Some have built-in fans and heaters that speed the composting process, and require electricity.

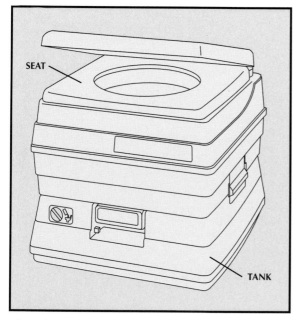

Chemical toilets.
Portable chemical toilets *(above)* are made in two parts. The tank detaches from the seat for emptying. The unit is then cleaned, disinfected, and refilled with the recommended products before being reused.

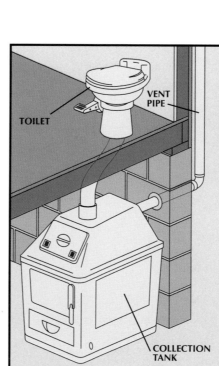

Composting toilets.
Composting toilets are available in two basic types. Large units *(above)* send waste into a collection tank installed outside the bathroom. These models have greater capacity than the smaller self-contained units *(photograph)*, which collect waste in trays underneath the seat. Both types need vent pipes to release gases and evaporating liquids.

Even small amounts of refuse and waste water from a cabin or cottage have to be disposed of with care—and by the method appropriate to the material. Waste involves a variety of different materials: the solid debris of day-to-day living, the liquids that drain from a sink, and the wastes from a toilet *(page 117)*.

Solid Waste: Lower the volume of household garbage by first composting all biodegradables. Depending on local codes, the remaining waste can be burned or hauled to a dump.

Waste Water Systems: In many regions, sanitary codes forbid the practice of emptying even waste water from a wash basin onto the ground. Frequently high in phos-phorus and grease, this water may contain food particles, bacteria, and viruses—substances that can pose a health hazard if they are not conducted safely away from dwelling places.

Before designing a water-disposal system, consult local health officials to determine the method required. Most sanitary codes call for a septic system *(page 120)*. In remote regions, smaller installations may be acceptable for occasional-use cabins—provided your soil can adequately absorb and filter the waste water you will generate. To test your soil, consult the U.S. Department of Agriculture extension service. If waste-water volume is fairly light and the drainage capacity of the soil is good, you may get approval to build a simple seepage pit *(below)* or an underground disposal bed *(opposite, top)*. An evapo-transpiration bed *(opposite, bottom)* may be permitted in areas of high temperature, low humidity, and poor drainage.

A Grease Trap: Any waste-water system you install must include a pretreatment tank, or grease trap, in which solids settle to the bottom and pipe-clogging greases float to the top before the water is dispersed by absorption or evaporation *(page 121)*. Locate the trap at least 50 feet from wells or streams, and at least 10 feet from the cabin and the property line. Inspect the trap periodically, remove large accumulations of grease and solids, and dispose of them properly.

 TOOLS

Keyhole saw
Shovel
Mason's trowel

 **MATERIALS**

30-gallon plastic
  garbage can
PVC pipe (2") and

fittings
Silicone sealant
Exterior-grade plywood ($\frac{3}{4}$")
Geotextile fabric

Sand
Precast concrete
  distribution box
Mortar

 **SAFETY TIPS**

Wear gloves and goggles when working with mortar.

FOUR BASIC SYSTEMS

A seepage pit.

In this system, waste passes from the house through an underground inlet pipe to a grease trap, which is a 30-gallon plastic garbage can buried up to its top *(page 121)*. Solids will settle to the bottom of the trap, congealed greases will rise to the top, and relatively clear waste water will trickle through the outlet pipe and into the pit, slowly filtering through the pit and into the surrounding soil. The inlet pipe is 2-inch PVC pipe attached to the cottage's waste-water outlet. The pit is dug 4 to 7 feet deep, 5 feet from the trap, and filled with irregularly shaped rocks. The outlet pipe runs underground from the trap, lies on a bed of rocks, and is covered with more rocks, geotextile fabric, and 6 inches of sand. The trap is covered with a patio-stone lid that can be lifted off to remove and properly dispose of the built-up grease.

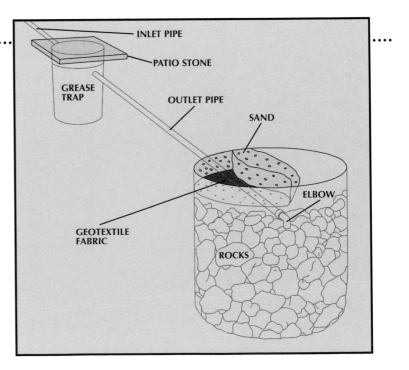

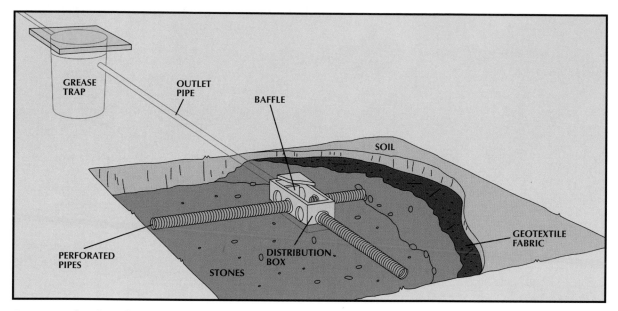

A network of underground pipes.

Here, waste water is distributed evenly through perforated pipes to the surrounding soil. From a garbage-can grease trap *(page 121)*, the waste water flows into a concrete distribution box *(page 121)* about 5 feet away, where its velocity is slowed by an internal baffle or wall in the box; the water is then channeled equally to 4-inch perforated pipes. Both the distribution box and the pipes are set level in a 3-foot-deep bed with a layer, at least 10 inches thick, of stones $\frac{3}{4}$ to 3 inches in diameter. The pipes are covered with at least 2 inches of stones, geotextile fabric, and an 8-inch layer of soil.

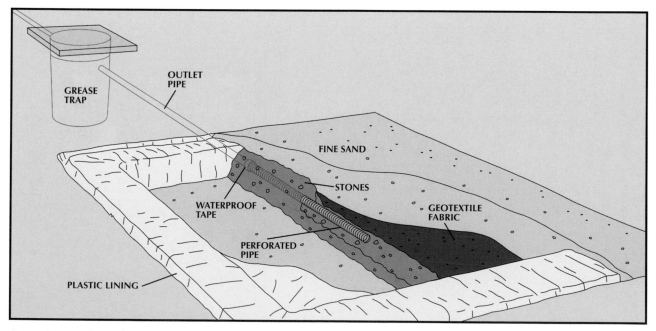

An evapo-transpiration bed.

Between $1\frac{1}{2}$ and 3 feet deep, this bed is lined with plastic sheeting to prevent water from seeping into the soil, and filled with fine sand. Waste water runs underground from a garbage-can grease trap *(page 121)* into a 2-inch perforated pipe that extends to the middle of the excavated bed; the pipe is surrounded by stones, covered with geotextile fabric, to prevent sand from blocking its perforations. Waterproof tape seals the area where the pipe enters the plastic liner. A bed that is used only in summer can be seeded with alfalfa to speed the evaporation process.

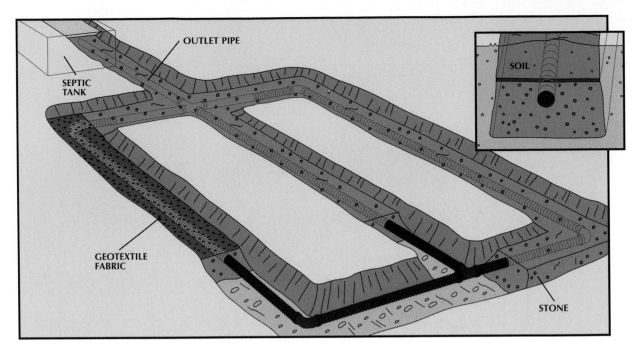

OUTLET PIPE

SEPTIC TANK

SOIL

GEOTEXTILE FABRIC

STONE

A septic tank with absorption trenches.

Waste water flows from the cabin through an underground pipe to the septic tank, where solids sink to the bottom, oils and grease float to the top, and gas escapes back through the inlet pipe to the cabin drain vent. The remaining liquid, called effluent, flows slowly out into the drainage bed. The septic tank is a large watertight box made of concrete, fiberglass, or plastic that will need to be delivered by truck and installed in a pit. The sizes of the tank and drainage bed depend on the number of bedrooms in the cabin or cottage and on local requirements. The bed is typically 4 to 6 inches deep. The outlet pipe from the tank is connected to a closed loop of perforated pipe with T-fittings and elbows. The pipe is laid in parallel trenches in the bed 6 to 10 feet apart, and 10 to 36 inches wide, dug $1\frac{1}{2}$ feet deep. In the trenches, the pipes rest on level beds of stones at least 6 inches thick. A layer of 2 inches of stone and geotextile fabric is placed on the pipes, and the fabric is covered with 4 to 6 inches of soil *(inset)*.

A WATER-SAVING TOILET

To conserve water and reduce the amount of effluence that seeps into the ground around your septic system, install a water-saving toilet. While standard flush toilets require gallons of water to push waste to a septic tank, a water-saving unit uses less than 1 quart. Standard plastic or copper tubing supplies water to the toilet, which connects to a 3-inch drainpipe that goes to the septic tank.

Maintaining Drainage and Septic Systems

✔ Mark off the location of the pipes and drainfield, and keep the area undisturbed. Don't drive or park cars over the system.
✔ Practice water conservation.
✔ Avoid pouring toxic chemicals into the drain.
✔ If the system has a grease trap, check it periodically and remove large accumulations that have risen to the top. For a septic tank, have a professional examine it regularly—typically every two to three years—and pump it out as needed.

With any system, have it inspected if you observe any of these signs:
✔ Slow draining of toilets or drains.
✔ Sewage odors.
✔ Lush growth over the drainfield.
✔ Sewage backup in the cottage or rising to the drainfield surface after heavy rains.

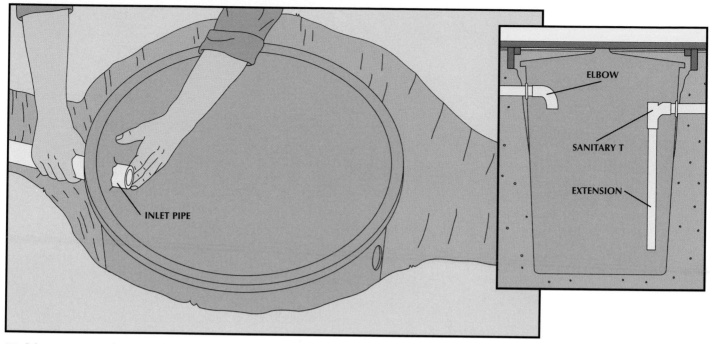

ELBOW

SANITARY T

EXTENSION

INLET PIPE

Making a grease trap.

◆ Cut holes into opposite sides of a 30-gallon plastic garbage can just below the rim. Make the holes slightly smaller than the 2-inch PVC inlet and outlet pipes, and place the inlet hole 1 inch higher than the outlet hole.

◆ Dig a level pit, set the can in it, and pack soil around the can.

◆ Dig one trench from the cabin to the inlet hole and another from the outlet hole to the drainage pit, sloping them $\frac{1}{4}$ inch per foot.

◆ Lay the inlet pipe in its trench and force the end into the hole in the can *(above)*. Fill gaps around the hole with silicone sealant and attach a 90-degree elbow to the end of the pipe.

◆ Insert and seal the outlet pipe in its hole and attach a sanitary T-fitting to the end of the pipe. To the fitting, fasten an extension that ends at least 5 inches above the bottom of the can *(inset)*.

◆ Place the lid on the can, pack the remaining space around the can with soil, and conceal the container with a $\frac{3}{4}$-inch exterior-grade plywood cover.

◆ Connect the outlet pipe to a pit, bed, or box *(pages 118-120)*, then cover the inlet and outlet pipes with geotextile fabric and 6 inches of sand.

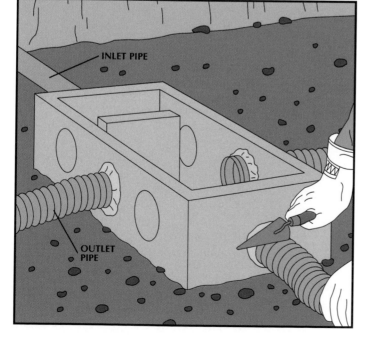

INLET PIPE

OUTLET PIPE

Sealing a tank or distribution box.

◆ Lay all the outlet pipes at the same level and the inlet pipe at least 1 inch higher to prevent the system from backing up—some codes require a septic-tank inlet pipe to be 3 inches higher than the outlet pipes.

◆ Prepare mortar from 60 percent Portland cement mix, 40 percent sand, and enough water to make the mix sufficiently stiff to stay on the joint after it is troweled on.

◆ Fill the spaces between the pipes and the box with chips of brick and trowel on the mortar *(left)*.

Modern woodburning stoves provide an efficient way to heat a small cabin or cottage. Though it may be tempting to restore a vintage stove for a rustic cabin, a new unit is actually a wiser choice.

Selecting a Stove: Advanced-combustion or catalytic models circulate and ignite volatile gases—burning these gases accounts for more than 50 percent of the heat from a wood fire in one of these stoves. The best modern stove can heat a cabin for the winter with half the wood required by an antique type.

Stoves are made of cast iron, sheet metal, or plate steel. Cast iron is the most expensive of the three, but lasts the longest and retains heat best. A dealer can help you choose the model most suited for your cabin or cottage.

Installation: Most stoves come with enough pipe to reach an 8-foot ceiling; the rest of the materials are purchased separately. Buy enough pipe to meet minimum height requirements (*page 124, Step 3*). For best results, place the stove in the middle of the cabin, but keep it at least 3 feet away from combustible materials. You can put it closer to a wall if you cover the wall with a heatproof shield; check codes on how to install the shield. Protect the floor under the stove as described below.

 TOOLS

Plumb bob
Electric drill
Utility knife
Saber saw

Hammer
Putty knife
Caulking gun
Screwdriver
Tin snips

 MATERIALS

Wood stove and stovepipe
Chimney pipe, support, and cap
Chimney pipe flashing

Roofing cement
Stovepipe finishing and trim collars
Common nails ($\frac{3}{4}$")
Roofing nails ($1\frac{1}{2}$")
Silicone caulk

 **SAFETY TIPS**

Wear goggles when operating a drill or driving nails; put on gloves when applying silicone caulk. Wear shoes with non-slip soles when working on the roof.

A typical installation.
This stove rests on a brick hearth set on a layer of sheet metal; the hearth extends at least $1\frac{1}{2}$ feet beyond the stove on all sides. The vent system begins at the flue collar, which holds the stovepipe in place. Just below the ceiling, this uninsulated pipe meets insulated chimney pipe that supports the pipe and protects the ceiling and roof from heat. Above the roof, flashing, a storm collar, and a chimney cap keep out rain and debris, and limit downdrafts.

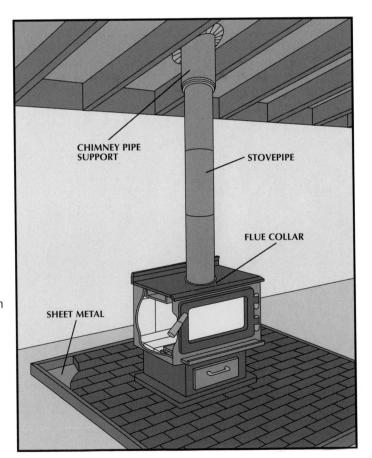

CHIMNEY PIPE SUPPORT

STOVEPIPE

FLUE COLLAR

SHEET METAL

1. Cutting the ceiling opening.

◆ With the stove in its final position, run sections of stovepipe from it to within 18 inches of the ceiling.

◆ Drop a plumb bob from the ceiling to the top of the pipe to mark the highest and lowest points where pipe will extend through the ceiling (right), then mark the ceiling at four additional points around the perimeter of the pipe.

◆ Remove the stovepipe sections, cover the stove with cloth or plastic, and drill a $\frac{1}{4}$-inch pilot hole through the ceiling at each mark.

◆ Subtract the stovepipe diameter from that of the chimney pipe, add 2 inches for clearance and, working on the roof, outline a circle to this distance outside the holes.

◆ With a utility knife, cut away the roofing material and roofing felt within the circle, then cut a hole through the roof sheathing with a saber saw.

STOVEPIPE

SUPPORT BRACKET

2. Installing the chimney pipe.

◆ Push the roof-support section of the chimney pipe down through the hole until the support brackets lie flat on the roof (left).

◆ Nail the brackets in place with $1\frac{1}{2}$-inch roofing nails.

◆ Add one section of chimney pipe to the support.

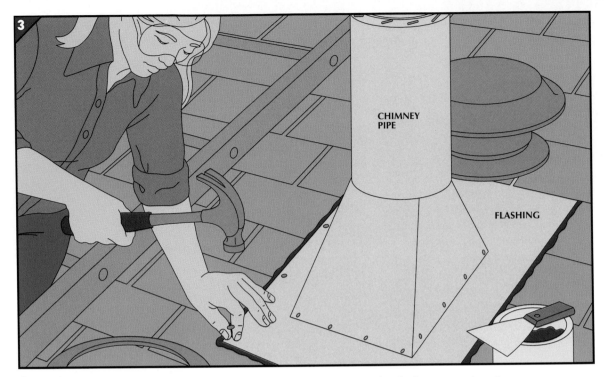

3. Installing the flashing.
◆ Fit the flashing over the chimney pipe, slipping its flanges under the shingles along the top edge, and outline it on the roof.
◆ Remove the flashing and spread roofing cement around the outline with a putty knife.

◆ Reposition the flashing over the pipe, press it into the roofing cement, then fasten it to the roof with 1½-inch roofing nails *(above)*.
◆ Add enough insulated pipe to the chimney pipe to extend the chimney 2 feet higher than any surface within 10 feet of it.

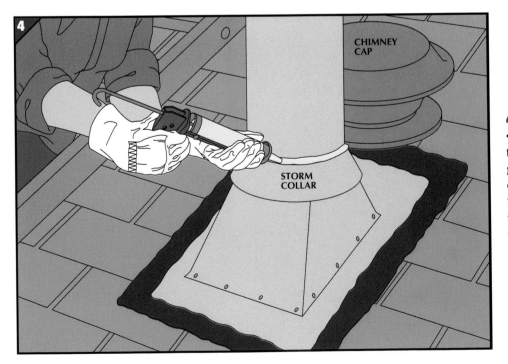

4. Putting on the storm collar.
◆ Fasten the storm collar around the top of the flashing and seal the gap between the collar and the chimney pipe with silicone sealant from a caulking gun *(left)*.
◆ Top the chimney pipe with a chimney cap.

5. Tying the pipes together.

◆ Secure the finishing collar partway down the stovepipe with setscrews, then push the top of the stovepipe up into the chimney pipe *(right)* and insert the bottom into the flue collar of the stove. If the stovepipe is too long, trim the top with tin snips.

◆ Loosen the setscrews on the finishing collar, slide it up to the bottom of the chimney pipe, and retighten the screws.

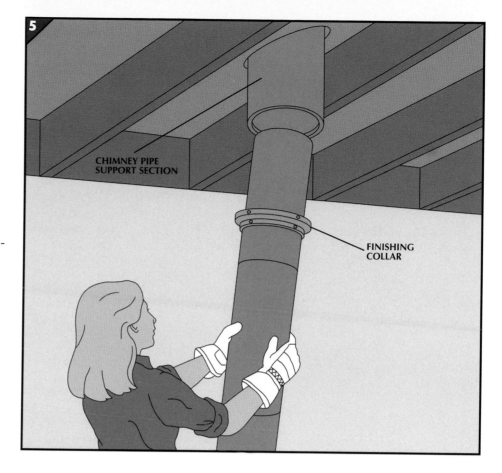

CHIMNEY PIPE
SUPPORT SECTION

FINISHING
COLLAR

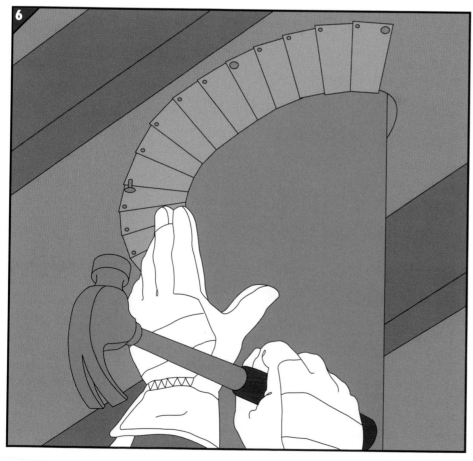

6. Putting on the trim collar.

For easy fitting and installation, a trim collar comes in sections that resemble a necklace of aluminum rectangles, loose at their inner edges. You may need two or three sections to make a full circle around a chimney pipe.

◆ Where the chimney pipe enters the hole in the ceiling, arrange the loose edges of a section of trim collar around the pipe and flush against the ceiling.

◆ Fasten the collar to the ceiling with a $\frac{3}{4}$-inch common nail in every fifth grommet *(left)*.

INDEX

TIME® LIFE BOOKS

Time-Life Books is a division of Time Life Inc.

TIME LIFE INC.
PRESIDENT and CEO: George Artandi

TIME-LIFE BOOKS
PRESIDENT: Stephen R. Frary
PUBLISHER/MANAGING EDITOR:
Neil Kagan

HOME REPAIR AND IMPROVEMENT:
Cabins and Cottages
EDITOR: Lee Hassig
DIRECTORS OF MARKETING: Steven
 Schwartz, Wells P. Spence
Art Director: Kate McConnell
Associate Editor/Research and Writing:
 Karen Sweet

Director of Finance: Christopher Hearing
Directors of Book Production: Marjann
 Caldwell, Patricia Pascale
Director of Operations: Betsi McGrath
Director of Photography and Research:
 John Conrad Weiser
Director of Editorial Administration:
 Barbara Levitt
Production Manager: Marlene Zack
Quality Assurance Manager: James King
Library: Louise D. Forstall

ST. REMY MULTIMEDIA INC.
President and Chief Executive Officer:
 Fernand Lecoq
President and Chief Operating Officer:
 Pierre Léveillé
Vice President, Finance: Natalie Watanabe
Managing Editor: Carolyn Jackson
Managing Art Director: Diane Denoncourt
Production Manager: Michelle Turbide

Staff for Cabins and Cottages

Series Editors: Marc Cassini, Heather Mills
Art Director: Robert Paquet
Assistant Editors: Jim Hynes, James
 Piecowye
Designers: Jean-Guy Doiron, Robert Labelle
Editorial Assistant: George Zikos
Coordinator: Dominique Gagné
Copy Editor: Judy Yelon
Indexer: Linda Cardella Cournoyer
Systems Coordinator: Éric Beaulieu
Technical Support: Jean Sirois
Other Staff: Linda Castle, Lorraine Doré,
 Liane Keightley

PICTURE CREDITS
Cover: Photograph, Robert Chartier.
 Art, Maryo Proulx.

Illustrators: La Bande Créative, Gilles Beau-
 chemin, Frederic F. Bigio (B-C Graphics),
 Roger C. Essley, Forte Inc., Gerry Gal-
 lagher, Adsai Hemintranont, Walter
 Hilmers Jr., Fred Holz, Judy Lineberger,
 John Massey, Peter McGinn, Joan S.
 McGurren, Eduino J. Pereira, Jacques
 Perrault, Raymond Skibinski, Jeff Swarts,
 Whitman Studio Inc.

The following illustrations are based on
 material from: 8: American Honda Motor
 Co., Inc. 64-65: Metal Roofing Sales.
 86: U.S. Geological Survey. 117 (left):
 Sanitation Equipment Ltd. 117 (center):
 Composting Toilet Systems Inc. 120
 (bottom): Sanitation Equipment Ltd.

Photographers: End papers: Glenn Moores
 and Chantal Lamarre. 9: Sears Craftsman.
 13: Glenn Moores and Chantal
 Lamarre. 14: MacKissic Inc. 16: Hoffco,
 Inc. 26: Glenn Moores and Chantal
 Lamarre. 46: Dewalt Industrial Tool Co.
 Inc. 61, 68, 70, 83: Glenn Moores and
 Chantal Lamarre. 87: Felker. 89: RCP
 Block and Brick. 106: Polyquip of Canada
 Ltd. 117: BioLet USA Inc.

ACKNOWLEDGMENTS
The editors wish to thank the following in-
dividuals and institutions: American Honda
Motor Co., Inc., Duluth, GA; APA-Engi-
neered Wood Association, Tacoma, WA;
Paul Armstrong, International Conference
of Building Officials, Whittier, CA; BioLet
USA Inc., Boston, MA; Brave Industries,
Inc., Annawan, IL; Stephen Bushway, Deer
Hill Enterprises, Cummington, MA; Century
Industries Inc., Little Rock, AR; Composting
Toilet Systems Inc., Newport, WA; DeWalt
Industrial Tool Company Inc., Mississauga,
Ont.; Felker, Olathe, KS; Louis V. Genuario,
Genuario Construction Co., Inc., Alexan-
dria, VA; Goodfellow Inc., Delson, Que.;
Guy Guenette Ltd., St. Laurent, Que.;
Hoffco, Inc., Richmond, IN; Kéfor Struc-
tures Ltée., St. Isidore, Que.; MacKissic
Inc., Parker Ford, PA; Metal Roofing Sales,
Sellersburg, IN; Polyquip of Canada Ltd.,
St. Laurent, Que.; Quadra Tools, Quathiaski
Cove, B.C.; RCP Block and Brick, Lemon
Grove, CA; Sanitation Equipment Ltd., Con-
cord, Ont.; Schroeder Log Home Supply
Inc., Grand Rapids, MN; Sears Craftsman,
Hoffman Estates, IL; Simpson Strong-Tie
Company Inc., McKinney, TX; Wally Swez,
Concord, Ont.; U.S. Geological Survey,
Golden, CO; Bob Wanke, Brookfield, WI;
Werner Co., Greenville, PA

Library of Congress
Cataloging-in-Publication Data
Cabins and cottages / by the editors of
 Time-Life Books.
 p. cm. — (Home repair and improvement)
Includes index.
ISBN 0-7835-3913-4
1. Log cabins—Design and construction—
 Amateurs' manuals. 2. Cottages—Design
 and construction—Amateurs' manuals.
I. Time-Life Books. II. Series.
TH4840.C33   1997
690'.837—dc21   97-38654